Puglia Travel Guide 2025

Where History Meets Hospitality: Embark
on an Unforgettable Adventure in Southern
Italy's Hidden Gem

Glen C. Flores

Puglia

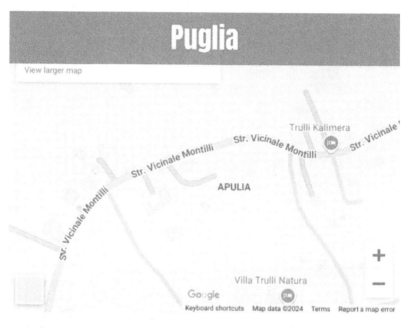

scan this QR Code

- Open your smartphone's camera app.
- Point the camera at the QR code.
- Hold steady until a notification appears.
- Tap the notification to open the link.
- Follow the instructions or view the content.

Copyright

Contents

Introduction

I vividly recall my first encounter with Puglian dirt the air was heavy with the aroma of sun-baked dirt and wild plants on a steamy July day. A surge of warmth swept over me as I got off the train at Lecce, the "Florence of the South," thanks to the sun and the kind grind of the residents. It was a long cry from the crowded piazzas of Venice or the busy streets of Rome. Keeping appeared to move more slowly here, in keeping with the Adriatic Sea's rhythmic lapping against the craggy shore.

The city's Baroque architecture, a symphony of elaborate detailing, whirling columns, and elaborate facades, instantly captivated me. Turning a corner unveiled a fresh work of art, each one more magnificent than the previous. The Basilica di Santa

Croce was a sight to see, with its ornate exterior and exquisite sculptures that told tales of dedication and faith. I discovered secret courtyards as I meandered around the winding cobblestone alleyways; each one was a peaceful haven among the hustle and bustle of the city. A neighboring bakery was releasing the perfume of freshly made bread, which blended intoxicatingly with the smell of jasmine in blossom.

When I left Lecce behind, I found myself in a country of opposites. I was taken to a world straight out of a fairy tale when I visited the Itria Valley, home of the famous trulli, conical-roofed cottages that adorn the countryside like quirky mushrooms. A photographer's paradise, Alberobello, a UNESCO World Heritage Site, has clusters of whitewashed trulli that create an enduringly beautiful sight. The town was painted in tone of gold and amber by the sun's extended shadows. As I went through its winding passageways, I couldn't help but feel at ease and at peace with the sound of my footfall resonating against the old stone walls. I ended up on the sun-drenched beaches of the Salento Peninsula, a little farther south. I was drawn to the Adriatic and Ionian Seas' glistening seas, which begged me to go swimming. The beaches provided a little piece of heaven for every taste, with some quiet and beautiful and others lively and busy. I lost track of the hours I spent discovering secret coves, soaking in the warm sunlight, and enjoying the simple joy of doing nothing.

However, Puglia offers more than simply breath-taking scenery. This area is rich in culture and history, as seen by the many old ruin sites scattered over the landscape. I was taken back to an era of gladiators and emperors when I visited the Roman Amphi theater in Lecce, a reminder of the rich history of the area. Tales of wars and conquests were spoken by the medieval fortress at Otranto, which was positioned on a rock overlooking the sea. Furthermore, I couldn't help but wonder about the cryptic function of the mysterious Castel del Monte, an octagonal stronghold covered in folklore.

A relaxing evening spent in a historic Masseria—a walled farmhouse transformed into a delightful hotel—is one of my favorite memories of Puglia. I was sitting on the patio enjoying a piece of orecchiette pasta with cime di rapa and a drink of the local Primitivo wine as the sun sank below the horizon, creating a warm light over the olive orchards. The sound of crickets chirping and the far-off laughter of kids playing in the courtyard filled the air. It served as a reminder of life's basic pleasures and a moment of absolute delight. Puglia is a sensory paradise where the old and new meld together harmoniously. It's a place of vivid hues, enticing aromas, and mouth-watering sensations. Time seems to slow down there, making it possible to appreciate each moment, form relationships with the locals, and make lifelong memories.

Puglia is the ideal location if you want to discover true Italian culture away from the hordes of tourists. Come and experience its cozy embrace, timeless treasures, and hidden jewels. Allow the water to calm your spirit, the sun to caress your skin, and the local cuisine to tempt your palate. Puglia is waiting to captivate you with its enchantment.

Are you prepared to set off on an amazing adventure across Italy's boot? Together, let's discover Puglia!

An overview of Puglia

Puglia, located in the southeast of the country, is the famous "heel" of Italy's boot-shaped peninsula. This sun-drenched area, which is bordered by the Adriatic and Ionian seas, offers a mesmerizing combination of ancient riches, lively culture, and natural beauty.

The coastline of Puglia is the longest of any Italian mainland area, and it provides a wide variety of scenery. There is a beach paradise for every tourist, from the breath-taking cliffs and secluded coves of the Gargano Peninsula to the immaculate sandy beaches of Salento. Inland, undulating hills covered with historic vineyards and olive groves provide a magnificent setting for quaint towns and villages.

The main cities in the area are all distinct from one another. The capital, Bari, is a lively place with a beautiful historic core. Known as the "Florence of the South," Lecce captivates with its tasteful Baroque architecture and sophisticated ambiance. The whitewashed cottages of Ostuni, often known as the "White City," glimmer as they tumble down a hillside.

The region of Puglia is speckled with enthralling towns and villages, each possessing a unique character. Alberobello, a UNESCO World Heritage Site, is famous for its recognizable Trulli. Polignano a Mare, situated on a limestone cliff, provides stunning views of the Adriatic Sea.

Puglia offers a remarkable voyage of exploration with its breath-taking coastline and rich cultural legacy.

Historical Background

Puglia's historical fabric, which reflects centuries of conquests, cultural exchanges, and strong communities, is as rich and diverse as its landscapes. Due to the region's advantageous position at the crossroads of the Mediterranean, several dynasties and civilizations have sought it out throughout history, leaving their lasting imprints on the region's people and terrain.

Historical Roots the Inception of Civilization: Puglia's history starts in the haze of prehistory when the Paleolithic period was when the first signs of human habitation were found. Early immigrants were drawn to the area by its rich resources and lush plains, and they founded prosperous settlements. The indigenous Messapian people, who originated from Illyria, were a powerful force during the Iron Age, leaving behind remarkable fortresses and unique pottery.

Greek Influence the Southern Frontier of Magna Grecia: Greek settlers came to Puglia's coast in the eighth century BC, establishing towns like Taranto and Metaponto. Magna Graecia, an era of thriving Greek culture and influence in southern Italy, began with this. Puglia developed into an essential component of this network, making contributions to the fields of philosophy, art, and architecture. The region's archeological treasures and the persistence of the Griko language—a dialect spoken by the descendants of ancient Greek settlers—are testaments to the heritage of Magna Graecia.

Roman Consolidation and Conquest: In the third century BC, Puglia came under the rule of the Roman Republic due to the emergence of Rome. Major routes like the Via Appia and the Via Traiana were built because of the region's strategic significance as a gateway to the eastern Mediterranean, facilitating commerce and communication. Urban towns grew and lucrative agricultural estates were established throughout the Roman era.

The Byzantine Period a Cross-Cultural Hub: The Byzantine era began in Puglia with the Western Roman Empire's collapse in the fifth century AD. There was instability for a while as the area was used as a battlefield by the Byzantines and other Germanic tribes. Byzantine art and architecture, however, left a lasting impression on the area and promoted a vibrant cultural interaction under their control. Magnificent examples of this creative heritage are the mosaics found in the Cattedrale di Otranto and the Basilica di San Nicola in Bari.

The Creation of a Kingdom after the Norman Conquest: Puglia was taken over by the Normans in the eleventh century under the command of Robert Guiscard, who established a strong kingdom that would determine the future of the area for decades. UNESCO has recognized the magnificent Castel del Monte as one of the magnificent castles and churches constructed by the Normans. There was also a time of comparatively stable and prosperous economic times under their control.

The Angevin and Swabian Dynasties: Puglia saw more political and cultural changes when the Swabian and Angevin dynasties succeeded the Norman Kingdom. In addition to power struggles and battles, the area saw a boom in literature, art, and architecture. Two examples of this period's architectural achievements are the towering Castello Svevo in Bari and the majestic Cattedrale di Trani, a masterpiece of Romanesque architecture.

Spanish Domination and Bourbon Restoration: Spanish authority over Puglia began in the sixteenth century and lasted for more than two centuries. While there was social upheaval and economic deterioration throughout this time, Lecce in particular is known for its spectacular fortifications and the creation of the unique Baroque architectural style. The Bourbon Restoration of the 18th century marked the beginning of a period of modernity and change.

Italy's Unification with Modern Times: Puglia actively participated in the 19th-century Risorgimento, an attempt to unite Italy. In 1861, the area was included in the newly established Kingdom of Italy. Significant obstacles, such as the destruction of World War II and economic hardship, were faced throughout the 20th century. But in the last few years, Puglia has become a more active and lively area, embracing its rich cultural legacy and paving the way for a successful and sustainable future.

Puglia Present-Day: Puglia is a living reminder of its rich and fascinating past. The architecture, customs, and landscapes of the area serve as monuments to the many civilizations that have influenced its identity. Puglia provides a fascinating trip through time, from the ancient remains of Magna Graecia to the Baroque splendors of Lecce. Because its people are so proud of their origins, they keep up with their customs, preserving Puglia's essence for future generations.

Culture and Traditions

Puglia's cultural environment is a fascinating fusion of vibrant festivals, age-old customs, and creative manifestations that honor the area's lasting spirit and rich heritage.

Festivals & Celebrations: Puglia comes alive with vibrant festivals all year long that highlight the region's enduring customs. During the Festa di San Nicola, Bari celebrates the city's patron saint with a spectacular fireworks show and huge procession. The lively music event, Notte della Taranta, in Otranto, honors the ancient Pizzica dance of the area, which is said to be able to heal spider bites.

Dance and Music: Puglian culture is deeply rooted in dance and music. The energetic and passionate Pizzica dance is backed by the rhythmic sounds of accordions, violins, and tambourines. The area also has a strong folk music heritage, with songs that have been handed down through the years often narrating stories of the sea, love, and grief.

Art and Craftsmanship: Puglia's numerous crafts and creative traditions bear witness to its artistic heritage. The region's talented craftsmen are on display in the elaborate papier-mâché works of Lecce, the hand-painted pottery of Grottaglie, and the woven baskets of the Itria Valley.

Local customs and way of life: The Puglian way of life is distinguished by a great feeling of hospitality, community, and a profound appreciation for life's little joys. Family get-togethers, slow dinners, and the evening passeggiata are beloved customs that strengthen ties between people and provide a feeling of place.

Gastronomy: Puglian culture revolves around food, and the region's rich agricultural heritage and maritime influences are reflected in the cuisine. Every dish, from the well-known orecchiette pasta to the velvety burrata cheese and the freshest fish, narrates a tale of love and tradition.

Religious Devotion: Puglian culture is strongly rooted in Catholicism, with a large number of churches, cathedrals, and religious celebrations influencing the area's spiritual climate. Puglia's deep religious beliefs are shown by the magnificent mosaics of the Cattedrale di Otranto and the Basilica di San Nicola in Bari, two important pilgrimage sites.

Puglia's customs, festivals, and creative manifestations make up a colorful and dynamic cultural tapestry. It is evidence of the area's tenacity, inventiveness, and strong ties to the past.

Why Visit Puglia?

Puglia has many attractive reasons to come, with its alluring mix of history, culture, and scenic beauty. The following are a few of the most alluring sights and activities that make this area a must-visit:

Genuine Italian Charm: With its laid-back vibe, friendly people, and focus on appreciating life's little joys, Puglia personifies "la dolce vita," or the sweet life. Take in the people's authentic hospitality, get fully immersed in their customs, and accept the slow pace of Puglian life.

Architectural Wonders: Puglia's architectural environment is a treasure trove just waiting to be discovered, from the famous Trulli of Alberobello, a UNESCO World Heritage Site, to the Baroque splendors of Lecce. Explore historic castles, Romanesque churches, and quaint whitewashed towns that evoke memories of bygone eras.

Beach Lovers and Water Enthusiasts will find a beachfront paradise in Puglia thanks to its long coastline. Enjoy the sun on immaculate sandy beaches, savor the crystalline waters of the Adriatic and Ionian seas, or discover secret coves and sea caves.

Culinary Delights: The cuisine of Puglia is a celebration of local, fresh products and long-standing customs. Savor the region's signature delicacies, including the finest fish and locally produced olive oil, as well as handmade orecchiette pasta and creamy burrata cheese.

Untouched Landscapes: Venture outside of the city to explore Puglia's magnificent natural landscapes. Explore the grottoes and secret caverns scattered around the coastline, go on a hike through the untamed grandeur of Gargano National Park, or go cycling in the charming Itria Valley.

Rich History and Culture: The Greeks, Romans, and Byzantines are only a few of the ancient civilizations whose strands are interwoven into Puglia's historical fabric. Explore the region's intriguing heritage by visiting archeological sites, medieval castles, and baroque cathedrals.

Festivals and Traditions: Take in Puglia's colorful festivals and cultural events. These festivities, which range from the Festa di San Nicola in Bari to the Notte della Taranta in Otranto, provide an insight into the joyous atmosphere and ingrained customs of the area.

Undiscovered Adventures: Escape from the throng and discover Puglia's hidden beauties. Discover lesser-known towns, go on a trip through isolated natural areas, or stumble across a quaint local marketplace. Those who wander off the usual path in Puglia are rewarded with remarkable experiences.

Warm Hospitality: Puglians are well known for their kindness and friendliness. Be greeted with wide arms and sincere grins at homes, restaurants, and stores to experience the essence of Italian hospitality.

Value for money: Puglia is quite affordable when compared to other of Italy's more well-known tourist sites. Savor tasty meals, reasonably priced lodging, and genuine experiences without going over budget.

Puglia is a place that is sure to charm and motivate travelers. Puglia has something for every kind of tourist, whether it is adventure, leisure, cultural immersion, or just a taste of real Italian living. Come experience the enchantment of this undiscovered jewel nestled in Italy's heel. You will not be let down.

Chapter 1: Practical information

Best time to go

The shoulder seasons, which are April through June and September through October, provide nice weather, fewer people, and the chance to participate in regional celebrations and festivities. Autumn offers pleasant weather and the abundance of the harvest season, while spring provides blooming wildflowers and colorful Easter festivities.

Summertime: July–August Puglia's summer is defined by hot, sunny days and active coastal towns, making it the perfect season for beach lovers and those looking for a lively environment. This is peak season, so be prepared for higher pricing and more people.

Winter (November–March): Although less well-liked, winter offers a special chance to see Puglia's more sedate side, with comfortable temperatures and fewer visitors. You'll save money and get a more personal experience, even if certain attractions can only be open for a short time or be closed.

Weather and Climate

Puglia has warm, dry summers and moderate, rainy winters characteristic of the Mediterranean region.

Summertime: June–August Anticipate long, bright days with average highs between 28 and 32°C (82 and 90°F). Because there is seldom rain, it is ideal for outdoor exploration and beach days.

April–May and September–October, or Spring and Autumn: 18–25°C (64–77°F) is a pleasant temperature range with occasional rains. Without the summertime crowds, these shoulder seasons are perfect for outdoor activities and tourism.

Winter (November–March): Generally mild, with highs of 10–15°C (50–59°F) and more frequent precipitation. Even though it's not beach weather, it's a perfect time to take in the vibrant culture and festive vibe of the area.

From June to October, the sea is warm enough for swimming, with peak summer temperatures of 25–27°C (77–81°F).

Keep in mind that Puglia is a big territory with many microclimates. The Salento Peninsula in the south is often warmer and dryer than the Gargano Peninsula in the north, which sees somewhat colder temperatures.

Entry and visa requirements

Puglia is part of Italy, so the conditions for admission and visas vary depending on your country, the reason for your visit, and how long you want to stay.

For visits up to 90 days within 180 days, citizens of the European Union (EU), the European Economic Area (EEA), and

Switzerland do not need a visa. You must have a current passport or national identification card.

For nationals of the US, Canada, Australia, New Zealand, and many other countries that have visa-waiver agreements with the Schengen Area:

- No visa is needed for stays up to 90 days within 180 days.
- It is necessary to have a valid passport that is at least three months valid beyond the anticipated stay.
- You could be required to provide documentation of enough money, lodging, and future travel.
- Travelers from countries where visas are not required will have to apply ahead of time for an ETIAS (European Travel Information and Permission System) travel permit as of November 2023. This is often good for three years and may be completed online.

Citizens of other countries will probably need a Schengen Visa.

- The particular kind of visa you need depends on why you are visiting (business, tourist, etc.).
- Well in advance of your travel, you must apply at the Italian embassy or consulate in your home nation.
- Normally, you'll need a valid passport, evidence of lodging, travel insurance, and enough cash.

Important Information:

- Before departing, always confirm the most recent visa and entrance requirements with the Italian embassy or consulate in your home nation, since they are subject to change.
- Make sure your passport is valid for at least three months after the day you want to enter the Schengen Area.
- When traveling, keep copies of your passport and other critical papers with you.
- You may need another kind of visa or permission if you want to remain in Italy for more than ninety days or reasons other than tourism.

Extra Sources:

Italian Ministry of Foreign Affairs and International Cooperation: https://www.esteri.it/en/

Schengen Visa Information: https://www.schengenvisainfo.com/

Notice:

- Requirements for entrance and visas are subject to change. Always check authoritative sources for the most recent information.
- This material is not legal advice; rather, it is meant to serve as a general guide.

Money and currency matter.

Currency: The Euro (€) is the accepted form of payment in Puglia and the rest of Italy.

Savings Advice:

- Puglia provides a selection of solutions to accommodate various price ranges.
- To save money on lodging and transportation, think about going in the shoulder seasons, which are spring or fall.
- For fresh and reasonably priced food, choose your local markets and grocery shops.
- Enjoy picnics in picturesque locations and take advantage of free events and attractions.
- For shorter trips, use public transit or think about renting a bike.

Exchange of Currency:

- Before leaving for your vacation, exchange money, or arrive at the airport.
- ATMs, which are commonly accessible and provide easy currency conversion, are referred to as "Bancomat" in Italy.
- Larger retailers, restaurants, and hotels all take credit cards.
- Bring cash for tipping at smaller businesses, markets, and other events.

Additional Tips:

- Before using your card overseas, find out about any international transaction fees from your bank.
- To prevent any problems with using your card, let your bank know about your trip schedule.
- If you are traveling, think about using a credit card that has no international transaction fees or rewards.

You may have an unforgettable and reasonably priced vacation to Puglia by paying attention to your expenditures and heeding this advice.

Getting Around

Puglia has a range of transportation choices to accommodate various tastes and travel patterns. Here's a summary to assist you get about the area:

Public Transport:

Trains: The most effective way to go from Puglia's big cities to its smaller communities is to take the train. The national rail network, which links Bari to locations like Lecce, Brindisi, and Foggia, is run by Trenitalia. Smaller towns and villages are served by the Ferrovie del Sud Est (FSE) network, which provides a picturesque ride through the countryside.

Buses: Local buses link smaller towns and cities that aren't serviced by railroads. Puglia is home to several bus companies, such as STP and Ferrovie del Sud Est (FSE). Although buses may be slower than trains, they are a more cost-effective choice and can go to far-flung locations.

Car Rentals:

Adaptability and Independence: Renting a vehicle gives you the best freedom to travel Puglia at your own pace, going off the main track and finding hidden treasures.

Drives along coastal roads and over rolling hills are the greatest ways to take in Puglia's stunning scenery and quaint communities.

Think about this: Parking at well-known tourist locations may be difficult, and traffic can become heavy in cities around rush hour.

Alternative Ways of Transportation:

Bicycles: Riding a bike is a common way to see Puglia's coastal and rural areas. Bike rentals are offered in several municipalities, and several places have designated bike lanes.

Motorbikes and scooters provide an additional means of independent transportation, especially when covering shorter distances and maneuvering through congested areas.

Taxis are a convenient door-to-door transportation alternative that is widely accessible in cities and villages.

Boat excursions and Ferries: Boat excursions and ferries provide beautiful views and access to secluded beaches as you explore Puglia's coastline and islands.

Advice for Traveling:

- Make a plan: In advance, check the timetables and available transit options, particularly for smaller towns and villages.
- Verify Tickets: To avoid penalties, make sure your bus or rail tickets are valid before boarding.
- Examine a Travel Pass: If you intend to use public transportation often, a travel pass can be more cost-effective.
- Drive carefully: Especially while driving in rural locations, pay attention to local driving customs and road conditions.
- Honor the environment: Whenever feasible, use environmentally friendly modes of transportation like public transit or cycling.

Navigating Puglia may be a memorable aspect of your trip with a little preparation and adaptability. Select the transportation options that best fit your requirements and tastes, then set off on an amazing adventure across this fascinating area.

Language and Communication

Official Language: Italian is the official language of Puglia and the whole country.

Languages of the Region and Dialects:

Although Puglia is home to several dialects and regional languages that represent its rich cultural past, Italian is the language that is generally spoken and understood there as well.

Among them are:

- Barese: A language spoken around Bari
- Foggiano: Speak in the region of Foggia
- Salentino is the dialect spoken in the Salento region.
- Griko: A dialect of Greek that is spoken in a few communities around Salento
- Arbëreshë: A dialect of Albanian spoken in some localities

Useful Phrases and Tips:

Basic Greetings:

- "Buongiorno" means "good day/morning."
- "Good evening," or "Buonasera"
- "Ciao" (informal for "Hello/Goodbye")
- "Grazie" means "thank you"

- "Prego" (thank you very much)
- Please, "Per favore"; "Scusi" (pardon me).

The Most Important Question:

- "Parla inglese?" (Are you able to speak English?)
- "Quanto costa?" (What is the price?)
- "Dove si trova...?" (Where is that?)
- "Mi può aiutare?" (Can you assist me?)

Additional Advice:

- Locals will appreciate you knowing even a few simple Italian words.
- Attempt speaking Italian; even if you can't pronounce it correctly, don't be frightened to attempt.
- Body language and gestures may also be useful in communicating.
- In particular, if there are language difficulties, use patience and civility.
- If you're having trouble communicating, think about using a phrasebook or translation tool.

Even if English is spoken in certain tourist locations, you will have a better time and show respect for the local way of life if you try to pick up a few Italian words.

Remember, that there is more to communication than simply words. A warm demeanor and a smile can help to bridge any language barriers.

Health and Safety

Maintaining your health and safety while traveling is essential to a worry-free and delightful stay in Puglia. The following are important health and safety reminders:

Vaccinations:

Regular vaccines: Make sure you have had all recommended vaccines, including the annual flu shot, varicella (chickenpox), diphtheria-tetanus-pertussis, measles-mumps-rubella (MMR), and polio.

Suggested Vaccinations: Discuss any extra shots, such as hepatitis A and B that may be advised for Italy with your doctor or a travel health clinic at least 4-6 weeks before your departure.

Medical Facilities:

Emergency Services: For immediate medical help, dial 112.

Pharmacies: Throughout Puglia, pharmacies, or "," are easily accessible. Pharmacists may guide over-the-counter treatments and mild illnesses.

Hospitals and Clinics: Puglia is home to a sizable number of both public and private facilities that provide high-quality medical treatment. If you have a medical emergency, ask your lodging for help or call the emergency services in your area.

Common Safety Measures:

Petty Theft: Take extra care with your possessions in busy places and popular tourist destinations. Refrain from carrying a lot of cash, and safeguard your valuables.

Scams: Keep an eye out for typical travel scams, such as phony petitions or diversion. Make use of trustworthy transportation providers and tour operators.

Road safety: Drive carefully and observe the local driving customs. In some places, roads may be twisting and narrow.

Sun Safety: There is a lot of sunlight in Puglia. Wear a hat, sunglasses, and sunscreen to protect yourself from the sun, particularly during the hottest parts of the day.

Water Safety: At beaches, heed the flags and warning signs. Don't swim by yourself; stick to the designated swim zones.

Travel Insurance: To cover unforeseen medical costs, trip cancellations, and misplaced baggage, comprehensive travel insurance is strongly advised.

Extra Advice:

- Keep a copy of your passport and any other necessary paperwork close at hand.
- In case of emergency, register with the Italian embassy or consulate in your country.
- When visiting places of worship, be mindful of regional traditions and wear modest clothing.
- Drink bottled water to stay hydrated, particularly in hot conditions.
- In a basic first aid kit, store basic first aid materials and medicines.
- Acquire a few emergency phrases in Italian.

By following these health and safety recommendations, you can reduce hazards and ensure a fun and safe vacation in Puglia. Keep in mind that safeguarding your well-being while traveling just requires a small amount of planning and attentiveness.

Chapter 2: Top Attractions

Alberobello and the Trulli

Alberobello is known for its distinctive trulli, conical-roofed limestone homes that resemble homes from a fairy tale and are recognized as a UNESCO World Heritage site. These quaint buildings, constructed without the use of mortar, demonstrate the locals' creativity and skill in dealing with the limited construction materials available in the area.

Key Attractions and Experiences:

- Rione Monti: Stroll around this charming neighborhood, where more than a thousand trulli line the twisting, narrow lanes. Explore the repurposed trulli stores, eateries, and lodgings to experience the enchanted ambiance.

- Trullo Sovrano: See this one-of-a-kind, two-story trullo, which is now a museum exhibiting local culture and traditional furniture.
- Church of St. Anthony: Take in the beauty of this little trullo church, which demonstrates the adaptability of this architectural design.
- Breath-taking views of the trulli-studded countryside may be obtained by climbing the hill to the Belvedere platform.

Useful Advice:

- The best times to visit are in the spring (April–May) and fall (September–October), when there are fewer tourists and excellent weather.
- Recommended Itinerary: Take a day trip to Alberobello, making time to explore the Trullo Sovrano, meander through the Rione Monti, and have a leisurely lunch or supper.
- Tours with Guides: If you'd want to know more about the trulli's background and design, consider taking a guided tour.
- Investigate with respect, keeping in mind that many trulli are still private residences. Admire them from the outside and only go inside the publically accessible ones.

Puglia's rich cultural legacy is exemplified by Alberobello's trulli, which provides a singularly captivating experience.

The Valley of Itria

Tucked away in the heart of Puglia, the Itria Valley is a mesmerizing scene of undulating hills, old olive orchards, and huge vineyards that weave a peaceful tapestry. The recognizable trulli of the valley, strewn over the landscape, provide a whimsical element to this picture-perfect scene.

Charming Town:

Locorotondo: Situated on a hill, this round town provides sweeping views of the valley. Explore its winding lanes, admire the pastel-colored homes decked with vibrant flowers, and visit the stunning Baroque church, Chiesa Madre San Giorgio.

Martina Franca Martina Franca, well-known for its exquisite Baroque architecture and lively cultural scene, is a pleasure to visit. Take in an evening of opera or classical music at the Teatro Verdi, and see the magnificent palace from the 17th century, the Palazzo Ducale.

Cisternino: This little village is well-known for its "fornelli pronti," which are butcher shops that cook the meat of your choice right there. Experience the warmth of its traditional ambiance, taste the delectable local food, and meander through its labyrinthine lanes.

Events and Activities:

Cycling: Ride your bike through the picturesque valley's landscape, passing past vineyards, olive groves, and trulli. You may choose to explore at your speed or take one of the several businesses' guided bike trips.

Hiking: Follow the paths that wind through woods, hills, and quaint towns to explore the natural beauty of the valley on foot.

Wine Tasting: Savor some of the famous wines from the area, such as the rich Martina Franca DOC and the fruity Locorotondo DOC. Take tastings and tours of the nearby vineyards.

Experience the elegance of a classic trullo while on vacation— many of which have been transformed into quaint guesthouses and vacation rentals.

Immerse yourself in Puglia's natural beauty, indulge in its delectable cuisine, and feel the warmth of its genuine culture in the Itria Valley, a tranquil getaway.

Bari

Bari, the dynamic capital of Puglia, is a place where modernism and tradition blend to create an alluring ambiance that attracts tourists. Discovering its historic core and taking in the vibrant cultural scene are just two of the many things this vibrant port city on the Adriatic coast has to offer.

Top Attractions:

Church di San Nicola: Containing the remains of Saint Nicholas, this imposing Romanesque church is a global Christian pilgrimage destination. Admire its magnificent mosaics, elaborate construction, and the crypt that holds the saint's relics.

Once a Norman stronghold, Castello Svevo is an impressive 12th-century fortress that provides a window into Bari's medieval history. Discover its majestic halls, courtyards, and ramparts while taking in expansive views of the city and the ocean.

Bari Vecchia, also known as Old Town, is the historic center of the city. Get lost in the winding lanes. Enchanting whitewashed homes, secret courtyards, and historic churches may all be found here. Don't pass up the chance to see the ladies from the area hand-make orecchiette pasta in the doorways.

Cultural Scene:

Bustling Markets: Take in the lively ambiance of Bari's markets, including the Mercato del Pesce, where you may eat fresh fish and regional goods.

Festivities: Immerse yourself in the rich cultural traditions of the city during its vibrant festivals, such as the Festa di San Nicola, a lavish celebration dedicated to the city's patron saint.

Tasty Cuisine: Food enthusiasts will be delighted by Bari's culinary scene. Savor the tastes of classic Puglian cuisine, such as fresh fish and olive oil that is produced nearby, orecchiette with cime di rapa (turnip greens).

Bari is a vibrant city that provides a distinctive fusion of modernity, culture, and history. Bari is certain to make an impact, whether you're taking in the sights at its historic sites, meandering through its busy marketplaces, or just soaking up the ambiance in its quaint old town.

Lecce

Known as the "Florence of the South," Lecce enthralls visitors with its opulent Baroque buildings and charming ambiance. Warm, honey-colored limestone from the area is used to create the elaborate façade, carved balconies, and expansive piazzas seen in the city's old centre.

Highlights of the architecture:

The most striking features of Lecce may be found around the Piazza del Duomo, the city's majestic center. The Duomo, or cathedral, is a masterwork of Baroque architecture with its high bell tower and elaborate exterior.

Basilica di Santa Croce: This well-known church is well-known for its ornately designed exterior, which is adorned with a multitude of statues, cherubs, and mythological animals. The area is made grander by the nearby Palazzo dei Celestini, which is now a government facility.

Roman Amphitheatre: Located in the centre of Lecce, this amphitheater offers a glimpse into the city's historic past. This surviving amphitheater used to be the site of many performances, including gladiatorial matches.

Taking in Lecce's Allure:

Explore the Historic Center on foot: Take in the colorful ambiance of the city as you meander through the winding alleyways and picturesque piazzas, all while appreciating the Baroque architecture.

Savor the Nightlife: With its bars, cafés, and restaurants bursting into the streets, Lecce comes alive at night. Take a nighttime promenade, or "passeggiata," and dine al fresco with the locals over an aperitivo.

Taste the Specialized food: Savor the mouth-watering food of Lecce, renowned for its tasty meals that are simple but packed with flavor. Try the "ciceri e tria" (pasta with chickpeas) or "pasticciotto," which are delicious pastries stuffed with custard, two of the region's delicacies.

Lecce is a must-see location in Puglia because of its distinctive combination of Baroque beauty, lively culture, and kind hospitality. Lecce will amaze you whether you're an enthusiast for architecture, a foodie, or just looking for a lovely Italian city to visit.

Ostuni

Ostuni is a sight to see, situated on a hill with a panoramic view of the Adriatic Sea. It is known as "La Città Bianca" (the White City) because of its maze-like labyrinth of alleys, steep stairs, and whitewashed dwellings. This beautiful village in Puglia is a must-visit location because of its stunning vistas and quaint medieval core.

Explore the Historic Centre:

- Explore the labyrinth of winding pathways to find secret courtyards filled to bursting with bougainvillea and vivid flowers.
- Admire the fine features of the whitewashed homes, with accents of bright blue framing their windows and doors.
- Climb the bell tower of the Cathedral, a magnificent specimen of Romanesque-Gothic architecture, for sweeping views of the town and surrounding landscape.

Enjoy Panoramic Views:

- Wander around the city walls and enjoy the stunning views of the Adriatic Sea and the surrounding olive trees.
- Locate a small café or eatery with a patio so you can enjoy a leisurely dinner while taking in the breathtaking view.

Day Trips:

- Beaches: Spend a day in the sun and sea by visiting the neighboring shoreline. Perfect beaches and glistening seas can be found at Torre Guaceto Nature Reserve, and Rosa Marina is a well-liked location for swimming and water sports.
- Itria Valley: Discover the quaint villages of Locorotondo, Cisternino, and Martina Franca, each of which has its personality and set of attractions.

Ostuni is a wonderful starting point for visiting Puglia's southern coast because of its scenic landscape, rich history, and proximity to beautiful beaches and quaint villages. Take in the sun on its neighboring beaches, get lost in its charming neighborhoods, and make lifelong memories.

Polignano a Mare

Polignano a Mare is a picturesque village that epitomizes Puglia's coastline splendor, perched steeply on limestone cliffs overlooking the turquoise waves of the Adriatic Sea. Its picturesque vistas, winding lanes, and whitewashed homes combine to create a unique environment.

Standouts:

Built on a series of cliffs, the town's unique location affords breathtaking views at every turn. As you stroll along the cliffside walks and explore the expansive terraces, enjoy the surrounding natural splendor.

At picture-perfect beaches, discover hidden coves and sandy sections nestled behind the cliffs. Cala Paura, Lama Monachile, and Cala Porto are well-liked locations for swimming, tanning, and taking in the pristine seas.

Gorgeous Old Town: Stroll around the maze-like lanes of the old center, which are dotted with whitewashed homes blooming with vibrant flowers. Discover the town's charming piazzas, Baroque churches, and laid-back vibe.

Grotta Palazzese: This unique restaurant set within a sea cave offers once-in-a-lifetime dining experiences. Savor delectable food while taking in the captivating Adriatic views.

Advice for Having Fun in Polignano a Mare:

- Swimming: Cool off with a swim in the Adriatic's crystal-clear waters. Take a thrilling leap down the cliffs into the water, or explore the many beaches and coves.
- Sunbathing: Take a seat in a quiet area on the rocks or unwind on the sandy beaches.
- Discovering the Old Town: Take in the town's laid-back vibe, meander around the historic centre's quaint streets, and find hidden gems.

- Evening stroll: Walk idly along the waterfront promenade as the sun sets and casts a mystical light over the town and the sea.

A Mare is an incredibly beautiful town in Puglia that offers a delightful combination of historical charm, natural beauty, and delicious food. This seaside village will win your heart whether you're looking for adventure, leisure, or just a taste of real Italian living.

Otranto

Nestled on the easternmost point of Italy's heel, Otranto is a mesmerizing seaside town that seamlessly blends natural splendor with historical significance. Because of its advantageous position, many conquests and cultural exchanges have occurred throughout the ages, creating a rich legacy of customs and history.

Key Attractions:

Aragonese Castle: With its commanding position above the Adriatic Sea, this majestic medieval fortification provides a window into the stormy history of Otranto. Investigate the towers, dungeons, and ramparts while imagining the conflicts and sieges that took place within.

Cathedral of Otranto: Witness Europe's most intricate mosaic floor in this 11th-century building. A masterwork of medieval art, the "Tree of Life" mosaic features biblical images and fantastical animals.

Beautiful port: Take a stroll around Otranto's quaint port, which is dotted with vibrant fishing boats and active eateries. Take in the town's laid-back vibe while watching the residents go about their daily lives.

Experiences:

Beaches: Take in the breath-taking coastline of Otranto, which has immaculate sandy beaches and glistening clean seas. The protected natural reserve of Baia dei Turchi is a well-liked location for swimming and tanning.

Boat Tours: To see the grottoes, sea caves, and secret coves scattered throughout the coast, take a boat tour. Take in the striking cliffs and Azure ocean from a different angle.

Summer Events: In the summer, Otranto comes alive with a plethora of festivals and events. One of the season's highlights is the lively music festival, Notte della Taranta, which honors the traditional Pizzica dance of the area.

Otranto is a very alluring location because of its unique combination of natural beauty, history, and culture. Otranto is certain to make an impact, whether you're taking in its colorful summer activities, unwinding on its immaculate beaches, or seeing its historic sites.

The Gallipoli

Puglia's Gallipoli is a charming seaside town that combines a lively beach lifestyle with old-world charm. Its old core is a treasure trove of winding lanes, Baroque churches, and an imposing castle that invites exploration and discovery. It is situated on a tiny island linked to the mainland by a bridge.

Historic District:

Coastal Charm Explore the labyrinth of cobblestone lanes, where bright flowers cover whitewashed cottages that make up a charming setting. Find little businesses nestled in quiet nooks, artisan workshops, and secret courtyards.

Baroque Churches: Explore the elaborate exteriors and interiors of Gallipoli's Baroque churches, such as the Church of Santa Maria della Purità and the Cathedral of Sant'Agata.

Discover the imposing Castello Angioino, a testament to the strategic significance of Gallipoli throughout history. Scale its towers to get sweeping views of the sea and town.

Beach Life:

Sandy Shores: Gallipoli is home to some of Puglia's most stunning beaches. Punta della Suina, Lido San Giovanni, and Baia Verde are well-liked locations for water sports, swimming, and tanning.

Gallipoli has a lot of beach clubs where you can hang out on sun loungers, drink drinks, and dance to the newest music.

Nightlife and Cuisine:

Nightlife: There are many bars, taverns, and clubs in Gallipoli that provide a variety of entertainment options. Take a leisurely walk along the coastal promenade, dance the night away at a fashionable club, or have a leisurely aperitivo in a piazza.

Specialties of Seafood: Savor the tasty and fresh seafood that is harvested every day by the local fisherman in Gallipoli. Sample the "," marinated fried fish specialty of the area, or have a seafood plate cooked at a beachfront café.

Gallipoli is a place where beach life, culture, and history all coexist together. Gallipoli provides an amazing experience in the center of Puglia, whether you're visiting its historic sites, relaxing on its beautiful beaches, or enjoying its delectable cuisine.

Matera (Destination Trip)

Matera is a beautiful city nestled into the craggy Basilicata region, only a short distance from Puglia. Matera is well-known for its historic cave homes, called the "Sassi," which have been inhabited since the Paleolithic period and are recognized as a UNESCO World Heritage Site.

Day trip from Puglia:

Transportation: A bus or rail from Puglia to Matera is an effortless journey. From Bari, the trip takes one and a half to two hours.

Suggested Schedule:

- Morning: After arriving in Matera, take a guided walking tour of the Sassi.
- In the afternoon, visit the cave churches and enjoy the expansive views from the Belvedere overlook.
- Evening: Indulge in a traditional dinner at a restaurant set within a cave while taking in the city's distinct ambiance.

Key Attractions and Experiences:

The Sassi: Explore the intricately designed streets of the Sassi while taking in the stunning views of the rock-cut cave homes. See Casa Grotta di Vico Solitario, a restored cave home that depicts the Sassi way of life.

Cave Churches: Explore the many frescoed and Byzantine art-adorned rock-hewn churches dotting the Sassi. The Church of Santa Maria de Idris and the Crypt of Original Sin are must-sees.

Panoramic Views: From the Belvedere perspective or the Piazza Duomo panoramic terrace, take in breathtaking views of the Sassi and the surrounding countryside.

Museums: Visit the National Archaeological Museum "Domenico Ridola" or the MUSMA (Museum of Contemporary Sculpture) to learn more about the history and culture of Matera.

Matera transports you back in time to a world of ancient cave houses and stunning surroundings, providing a memorable experience. From Puglia, a day excursion offers a peek into this remarkable city; to experience its enchantment, try staying overnight.

Castel Del Monte

A mysterious marvel of medieval architecture, Castel del Monte rises like a mirage from the Puglian landscape. Built by the Holy Roman Emperor Frederick II in the 13th century, this octagonal fortress is a UNESCO World Heritage Site that never fails to enthrall and amaze guests with its unusual layout and enigmatic function.

Wonder of Architecture:

Octagonal Pattern: The castle stands out from other medieval fortresses due to its unusual octagonal design, which has eight towers at each corner. Frederick II's passion for mathematics and astronomy is reflected in its geometric perfection and harmonious proportions.

Symbolism & Mystery: There is still much to learn about the symbolism and function of the castle. There are several theories about it, such as whether it is a hunting lodge, an astronomical observatory, or even a picture of the Holy Grail.

Practical Information:

Opening Times:

- 10:15 a.m. to 7:45 p.m., March through September
- 9:45 a.m. to 6:45 p.m., October through February
- January 1st and December 25th are closed.
- Adult admission fees are €10; EU citizens 18 to 25 pay €2, while minors under 18 and EU citizens 65 and above are admitted free of charge.

Transportation:

- By car: The castle is conveniently located close to the town of Andria.
- Public Transportation: Although the timetable may be restricted, buses go from Andria to Castel del Monte.

Beyond the Castle:

Discover the Countryside: You may go hiking, biking, and horseback riding amid beautiful scenery in the neighboring countryside.

Explore Adjacent Towns: During your stay, explore the quaint towns of Andria, Trani, or Corato; each has its own historical landmarks and distinctive attractions.

Emperor Frederick II was a man ahead of his time, and Castel del Monte is a monument to his ambition and vision. It is a must-visit location in Puglia because of its mysterious beauty and historical importance.

Chapter 3: Accommodations

Luxury Hotels and Resorts

Amidst the breathtaking scenery of Puglia, luxurious lodgings provide a unique combination of luxurious comfort and genuine encounters.

Borgo Egnazia (Savelletri di Fasano): With its courtyards, piazzas, and whitewashed houses, this sprawling resort is modeled like a typical Puglian town. It has an opulent spa, many pools, fine dining options, and a private beach club. Price Range: Expensive, drawing discriminating tourists looking for a lavish and engrossing experience.

In Savelletri di Fasano, Masseria Torre Maizza is a magnificently renovated 16th-century farmhouse that has been turned into an opulent hideaway. It offers classy accommodations, a fine dining restaurant, an amazing pool, and a private beach club. Price range: Expensive, suited for families and couples looking for a fusion of contemporary elegance and heritage.

Set beneath a 15th-century watchtower, Masseria San Domenico (Savelletri di Fasano) is a luxury establishment that provides a distinctive fusion of contemporary comfort and historical charm. It has a golf course, private beach access, thalassotherapy treatment, and roomy accommodations. High-end, perfect for golfers and anyone looking for a restful and refreshing getaway.

Nestled in a renovated 18th-century palace, the chic Paragon 700 Boutique Hotel & Spa (Ostuni) provides a unique fusion of modern amenities and historic allure. It has a gourmet restaurant, an opulent spa, and a rooftop pool. Price Range: Expensive, ideal for lovers of design and couples looking for a classy and private setting.

The Furnirussi Tenuta in Carpignano Salentino is a posh hideaway within a medieval estate bordered by vineyards and olive trees. It has tasteful accommodations, a Michelin-starred restaurant, a pool, and a variety of outdoor pursuits. Cost: Expensive; perfect for people looking for a quiet getaway and a fine dining experience.

These are just a few of the many upscale lodging options that Puglia has to offer. You may choose from a variety of accommodations, including chic boutique hotels, expansive resorts, and old-world materials, to ensure an amazing experience.

Boutique Hotels and Guesthouses

When it comes to small settings, individualized service, and distinctive experiences that encapsulate the spirit of the area, Puglia's boutique hotels and guesthouses provide a fascinating alternative to bigger resorts.

Located amid Lecce's historic district, the chic La Fiermontina Urban Resort provides 16 uniquely designed rooms and suites that combine modern amenities with regional accents. Savor fine dining at the on-site restaurant, unwind in the peaceful courtyard garden, and take advantage of the rooftop terrace. Price Range: Expensive, perfect for discriminating tourists and couples looking for a classy and exclusive experience in the center of Lecce.

Situated in an olive grove and housed in a beautifully renovated 16th-century farmhouse, Masseria Cervarolo (Ostuni) is a serene getaway just a short drive from the city. The facility has a restaurant offering traditional Puglian cuisine, a spa, and a swimming pool. Its 12 rooms are charmingly adorned with antiques and local artwork. Cost: From mid-range to high-end; ideal for families and couples looking for a peaceful and genuine rural experience.

Amid Monopoli's historic district is the sophisticated boutique hotel, Palazzo Guglielmo, which dates back to the 17th century. Each of the ten specially designed rooms and suites combines classic elements with contemporary conveniences. Savor your morning meal on the seafront rooftop terrace while taking in the quaint town's streets and charming harbor. Cost: From mid-range to high-end; perfect for couples and individuals looking for a chic and convenient location in Monopoli.

Corte Altavilla Relais & Charme (Conversano): This boutique hotel provides a mix of contemporary luxury and heritage, housed in a 15th-century palace. The 12 well-decorated rooms and suites have vaulted ceilings and unique frescoes. Indulge in fine dining at the on-site restaurant, unwind in the courtyard garden, and take in town views from the rooftop terrace. Price Range: Expensive, ideal for sophisticated tourists and couples looking for a classy and authentic Conversano experience.

Le Capase (Alberobello): At this little hotel in the center of Alberobello, discover the enchantment of lodging in a trullo. Its six distinctively styled trulli rooms provide a unique and genuine experience. Savor breakfast on the patio, stroll through the charming alleys of the town, and unwind in the garden. Price range: Mid-range, perfect for travelers looking for a special and romantic experience in Alberobello, especially couples.

These are just a few of Puglia's many, enchanting, and distinctive boutique hotels and guesthouses. Conscientious travelers may have an unforgettable and unique experience with them because of their intimate surroundings, customized treatment, and meticulous attention to detail.

Masserie (Farmhouses)

Staying in a Masseria—a tastefully remodeled farmhouse that provides a distinctive mix of rustic charm, contemporary conveniences, and tranquil surroundings—will allow you to experience Puglia in all its authenticity. Once the hub of agricultural activity, these ancient estates have been painstakingly transformed into warm lodgings that provide a peaceful respite from the daily grind.

Take in the breath-taking views of scented citrus orchards, vineyards, and olive groves as you lose yourself in the perfect countryside. Many masserie enable you to fully relax and experience the tastes of Puglia with their beautiful swimming pools, spas, and on-site farm-to-table restaurants.

Suggestions:

Nestled between old olive fields, Masseria Montenapoleone (Pezze di Greco) is an 18th-century Masseria that provides a serene haven with exquisitely furnished rooms, a swimming pool, and a restaurant that serves traditional Puglian cuisine. Cost from moderate to luxurious.

Surrounded by vineyards, Masseria Potenti (Manduria) is a 16th-century fortified farmhouse that offers a distinctive fusion of contemporary luxury and history. It has chic accommodations, a spa, a pool, and a Michelin-starred restaurant serving the best local cuisine. Cost is Expensive

Set in a 16th-century olive mill, Masseria Il Frantoio (Ostuni) is a quaint masseria that provides a polished but rustic experience. The facility has an organic restaurant, a spa, and a swimming pool. The rooms are furnished with traditional furniture and locally created artwork. Cost from moderate to luxurious

Nestled between olive trees and just a short distance from the coast, Masseria Torre Coccaro (Savelletri di Fasano) offers an opulent getaway. It has many restaurants for fine dining, a spa, a private beach club, and luxury accommodations. Cost is expensive

A stay at a Masseria provides an amazing experience in the center of Puglia's beautiful countryside, whether you're looking for a calm retreat, a romantic getaway, or a family holiday.

Trulli Stays

Sleeping in a Trullo, one of Puglia's famous conical-roofed homes, is an unusual experience. With their whitewashed exterior and rustic interiors, these quaint stone buildings provide a window into the area's rich architectural past.

Places:

Alberobello: The hub of trulli, where these charming homes make up whole communities. Numerous Trulli hotels, guesthouses, and vacation rentals are available; many of them provide contemporary amenities while maintaining the area's classic beauty.

Itria Valley: For a private and romantic retreat, explore the charming landscape with its strewn trulli.

Locorotondo: This little village has several Trulli lodging options that allow you to enjoy the allure of these unusual buildings while soaking up the lively vibe of the area.

Experiences:

- A light wind blowing through the olive trees, and the sound of birds singing as you wake up.
- Savor breakfast on a sun-filled patio with a view of the scenery dotted with trulli.
- Enjoy stargazing on your rooftop patio throughout the night.
- Explore the surrounding countryside by foot or on a bike, discovering secret pathways and quaint communities.

Price Range and Target Market:

- From budget-friendly guesthouses to opulent villas, trulli lodgings provide something for every taste.
- They are perfect for anybody who wants to fully immerse themselves in Puglia's genuine charm, families searching for a unique experience, and couples looking for a romantic getaway.

A Trullo sleep is an enchanting experience that lets you appreciate Puglia's natural beauty and rich tradition. This is a chance to go back in time and enjoy the little joys of living in this charming area.

Budget-Friendly Options

Puglia has a range of reasonably priced lodging alternatives for visitors looking for value and economy, letting them take in the beauty of the area without going over budget.

Hostels:

- Ostello Bello (Bari): This chic hostel in the center of Bari has cozy private rooms and dormitories, a rooftop patio, a shared kitchen, and planned activities.
- The Aia (Lecce): Located in the ancient town of Lecce, this inviting hostel offers clean rooms, a communal kitchen, and a pleasant ambiance in a restored historic structure.

Bed and breakfasts, or B&Bs:

- Le Terrazze (Polignano a Mare): This little B&B, which is close to the beach, offers breathtaking views of the sea. It provides cozy accommodations, a delicious breakfast, and a welcoming host.
- Bed and Breakfast Antica Dimora (Ostuni): This classic B&B offers a warm and genuine experience and is located in the core of the city's historic district. It offers cozy accommodations, a home-cooked breakfast, and a kind greeting from the proprietors.

Facilities for Camping:

Near the stunning beaches of Torre Rinalda, Camping Torre Rinalda (Lecce) has a variety of sites for tents, caravans, and camper vans in addition to mobile homes and villas. A restaurant, a swimming pool, and planned events are among the amenities.

Camping La Masseria (Gallipoli): This campground, which is close to Gallipoli in a tranquil rural area, has large pitches, spotless amenities, and a swimming pool. It's a fantastic choice for those who like the outdoors and families.

Extra attention to detail:

- Make a reservation in advance: It's best to reserve your lodging well in advance during the busiest travel months of July through August, particularly for hostels and well-liked campgrounds.
- Location: Consider how your lodging will relate to the scheduled activities and available transportation.
- Facilities: While campsites may provide a greater variety of amenities, hostels, and B&Bs sometimes just provide the most basic ones.
- Evaluations: To obtain a feel of the ambiance, hygiene, and value of each choice, read online evaluations left by previous visitors.

You can stretch your vacation budget and have a longer, more satisfying stay in Puglia if you choose affordable lodging.

Chapter 4: Dining and Cuisine

Culinary Traditions

Simple, fresh ingredients are celebrated in Puglian cuisine and turned into meals that are flavorful and healthful. It provides a distinctive and remarkable gastronomic experience, molded by the region's agricultural bounty and seaside setting, and deeply steeped in tradition.

Essential Components:

- Extra virgin olive oil, often known as the "liquid gold" of Puglia, is the base for many recipes, giving them depth and richness of taste.
- Puglia is well-known for its durum wheat, which is used to create a range of pasta forms, such as the well-known orecchiette.
- Vegetables: Puglian cuisine makes extensive use of seasonal, fresh vegetables such as peppers, eggplant, zucchini, and tomatoes.
- Seafood: A wide range of fresh seafood, such as mussels, clams, octopus, and fish, may be found in the Adriatic and Ionian waters.
- Dairy: Puglia is known for its mouthwatering burrata, mozzarella, and ricotta forte cheeses.

- Legumes: A mainstay of Puglian cuisine, chickpeas, lentils, and beans provide meal structure and nutrition.

Influences and Flavors:

- Mediterranean: Fresh herbs, garlic, lemon, and olive oil are highlighted in this cuisine, which embodies the region's characteristics.
- Simplicity: In many dishes, simple preparation methods let the quality of the ingredients take center stage.
- Tradition: The region's culinary legacy has been preserved over the decades via the transmission of several recipes.
- Influences: Throughout history, the cuisine has been shaped by a multitude of civilizations, including Greek, Roman, Arab, and Spanish, creating a distinctive and varied culinary scene.

A reflection of the region's rich agricultural and cultural legacy is seen in Puglian cuisine. It provides a taste-bud-pleasing, soul-nourishing sensory experience that leaves a lasting effect on everyone who partakes in it.

Must-Try Dishes

The food scene in Puglia is a veritable gold mine of tastes, with a wide variety of dishes that highlight the region's illustrious culinary past. These ten classic meals are a must-try when visiting:

Orecchiette with Cime di Rapa: Sautéed turnip greens, garlic, chili flakes, and anchovies are combined with ear-shaped orecchiette pasta in this traditional Puglian pasta dish. It's available in authentic trattorias across the area, but particularly in Bari.

Burrata: Made from cream and mozzarella, this fresh, creamy cheese is a real treat. Savor it with fresh tomatoes and basil, or add a splash of olive oil and sea salt. Look for it in the Andria and Corato districts, especially at the cheese stores and local markets.

Panzerotti: A common street food snack, they are deep-fried turnovers stuffed with mozzarella and tomato sauce. In Puglia, particularly in the Salento area, you may get them in bakeries and street sellers.

Fave e Cicoria: A distinct and gratifying blend of tastes is achieved when mashed fava beans are combined with bitter chicory leaves in this substantial meal. In the Itria Valley, try it in classic eateries.

Tiella Barese: Layers of rice, potatoes, mussels, and tomatoes are cooked to perfection in this baked dish. This traditional Bari dish is often served at family-owned trattorias and seafood restaurants.

Scapece: Fish marinated in vinegar, saffron, and breadcrumbs is fried and served in this classic meal. This is a zesty and tasty appetizer that is often available in seaside communities such as Gallipoli.

Pasticciotto: A popular breakfast or dessert dish, this sweet pastry is filled with a creamy custard. Pastry shops and bakeries in Puglia, especially Lecce, sell it.

Cartellate: A Puglian Christmas custom, these delicate pastries shaped like roses are sprinkled with honey or "vincotto" (cooked wine). During the holidays, look for them in bakeries and marketplaces.

Bombette Pugliesi: Perfectly cooked little pig buns stuffed with cheese, pancetta, and herbs. They can be tried at grilled meat-focused restaurants or butcher shops in your area.

Fresh Seafood: Because of its long coastline, Puglia has an abundance of fresh seafood. At beachside eateries and trattorias, savor grilled fish, pasta dishes with seafood, or a simple plate of raw seafood.

These are just a few of the many delectable foods that Puglia has to offer. Savor the delights of this culinary heaven, be daring, and explore the neighborhood's markets and eateries.

Olive Oil

Producing almost 40% of Italy's total olive oil production, Puglia is without a doubt the olive oil centre of the nation. The region's "liquid gold" permeates its veins, influencing its gastronomy, culture, and topography.

Reasons for its notoriety:

- Ideal environment: Puglia's Mediterranean climate, with its long, hot summers and mild winters, is ideal for olive tree growth.
- Ancient Olive Groves: The area is home to enormous tracts of old olive groves, some of which date back hundreds of years. These groves give the oil its distinct taste and character.
- Varietal Diversity: A vast array of olives, each with unique qualities, are cultivated in Puglia, leading to a varied selection of olive oils.

Key Varieties & Tasting Tips:

- Coratina: This vigorous type produces an oil with a strong, peppery flavor and a somewhat bitter aftertaste due to its high polyphenol concentration. Perfect as a drizzle over meats, grilled veggies, or thick soups.
- Ogliarola Barese: This oil is ideal for salads, seafood dishes, and dipping bread because of its light taste and subtle, fruity scent.
- Peranzana: This oil goes well with fresh cheeses, white meats, and vegetable dishes because of its green undertones and mild bitterness.

Taste Tips:

- Transfer a little quantity of oil into a glass and slowly warm it between your palms.

- After swirling the glass, take a deep breath to release the scents.
- Sip a little, allowing the oil to spread over your tongue.
- Have you noticed any fruity, grassy, herbaceous, or spicy flavors?
- Observe the aftertaste; is it smooth, aromatic, or bitter?

You may enhance your cooking experiences by discovering a world of tastes and sensations by delving into Puglia's olive oil types. Don't pass up the chance to see the olive oil mills in the area, see how it's made, and taste the "liquid gold" that makes Puglia unique.

Wine

The wine industry in Puglia is undergoing a resurgence as more and more growers create outstanding wines that highlight the region's distinctive terroir and native grape varietals. Puglia has a wide variety of tastes to satisfy any wine aficionado, from bold reds to crisp whites and pleasant rosés.

Notable Types of Grapes:

- Primitivo: The star of Puglian wine country, this robust red grape is prized for its high alcohol concentration and rich, jammy aromas. It excels at the well-known Primitivo di Manduria DOC.
- Negroamaro is another popular red grape that produces wines with a robust body and earth, spice, and black fruit

flavors. Seek out the Salice Salentino DOC, the home of the mighty Negroamaro.

- Nero di Troia: With notes of tobacco, leather, and blackberries, this old grape variety produces structured, rich red wines. Explore its possibilities in Castel del Monte's DOC.
- Verdeca, the most popular white grape, produces crisp, flowery, and citrus-flavored wines. View the Locorotondo DOC's range of applications.

Wineries and Wine Regions:

Peninsula of Salento: Some of Puglia's most renowned wines are produced in this sun-drenched area, which is home to the Salice Salentino and Primitivo di Manduria DOCs. See wineries such as Feudi di San Marzano, Cantine Due Palme, and Leone de Castris.

Valley of Itria: Known for its white wines, especially the DOC Locorotondo, this idyllic valley is home to many little vineyards. Investigate manufacturers like Cantine Menhir, I Pastini, and Cantina Cardone.

Castel del Monte: Nero di Troia is the star of the Castel del Monte DOC, which is located in close proximity to the famous castle. Visit vineyards such as Villa Schinosa, Rivera, and Torrevento.

Wine Experiences and Tours:

- Guided Wine Tours: Take a guided wine tour to see Puglia's vineyards and wineries, discover how wine is made, and sample a range of regional wines.
- Wine Tastings: A lot of vineyards provide tastings so you may try their wines and buy your favorites.
- Food & Wine Pairings: Savor a gastronomic adventure that pairs the best wines from the area with Puglian food.

Puglia's emerging wine sector provides a pleasant voyage of discovery, whether you're an experienced oenophile or just like a delicious glass of wine. Salutations!

Dining Experiences

Puglia's eating scene offers a wide range of experiences that highlight the region's culinary quality, catering to all interests and budgets.

Michelin-starred Restaurants:

Angelo Sabatelli (Putignano): Under the direction of famous chef Angelo Sabatelli, this two-Michelin-starred eatery serves a sophisticated tasting menu that combines regional specialties with cutting-edge cooking methods and global inspirations. A very remarkable culinary adventure awaits you.

Trani Quintessenza: This Michelin-starred restaurant, which is tucked away in the little seaside town of Trani, has a cuisine that highlights the best seafood the area has to offer, cooked with skill and devotion. The eating experience is enhanced by the refined surroundings and excellent service.

Trattorias Run by Families:

Run by the same family for generations, L'Antica Locanda di Piero (Ceglie Messapica) is a well-liked trattoria that provides genuine Puglian cuisine prepared with care using regional products. Their grilled meats and handmade pasta are not to be missed.

La Cucina di Mamma Elvira (Bari): Enter this welcoming trattoria in the heart of the city's historic district and you'll instantly be transported to a Puglian grandmother's home. Savor hearty, delicious meals such as braised meats and orecchiette with tomato sauce.

Perched on the cliffs overlooking the Adriatic, Da Tuccino (Polignano a Mare) is a family-run restaurant with stunning views and a cuisine that highlights the finest seafood.

Other Worthwhile Options:

Masseria Restaurants: A lot of masseries (farmhouses) now have great restaurants offering farm-to-table food. Try the grilled octopus or the famous "spaghetti alla Tuccino." In a cozy, rustic setting, enjoy classic cuisine and the finest ingredients.

Seafood Restaurants by the Sea: There are a lot of restaurants with delicious seafood meals and breathtaking sea views along Puglia's coastline. Seek for those that specialize in regional seafood and customary cooking methods.

Puglia's dining scene is likely to please your taste and leave you wanting more, whether you're looking for a Michelin-starred experience or a relaxing lunch at a family-run trattoria.

Cooking Classes and Food Tours

To strengthen your bond with the region's food culture, Puglia offers a variety of immersive culinary experiences in addition to restaurant meals.

Orecchiette-Making Classes: Where: Bari, Lecce, Alberobello, among other places. Experience: Learn from the neighborhood "nonnas" (grandmothers) how to make orecchiette pasta by hand. Form the dough into the well-known "little ears" and enjoy the results of your hard work with a delectable dinner.

Olive Oil Tastings and Farm Visits: Where: In Puglia's olive oil-producing areas, including Salento and the Itria Valley. Experience: Take a tour of olive gardens, see olive oil extraction, and taste a variety of oils to learn how to differentiate between their distinct tastes and scents.

Cooking Classes in Masserie: Location: Several Masserie, or farmhouses, provide culinary lessons; the Itria Valley and Salento are popular destinations. Experience: Savor a convivial supper with other participants while learning to cook traditional dishes with fresh, in-season ingredients. Dive deeply into the culinary traditions of Puglia.

Food and Wine excursions: Location: Bari, Lecce, and Ostuni are just a few of the towns and cities that provide guided food and wine excursions. Experience: To have a better understanding of Puglia's gastronomic and viticultural legacy, visit vineyards and wineries for tastings, peruse local markets, and try local delicacies.

Bari, Lecce, and other important cities are the locations for street food tours. Experience: Take a guided tour of the city's historic core, stopping at neighborhood stores and street food sellers to taste regional specialties and discover their cultural and historical importance.

These all-encompassing culinary adventures provide a special chance to learn more about Puglia's gastronomic heritage and create lifelong travel memories.

Chapter 5: Nightlife and Entertainment

Bari's Bars and Clubs

Bari's nightlife scene is vibrant and offers a wide range of alternatives to satisfy every taste. The city comes alive when the sun sets, turning into a haven for night owls with pubs, clubs, and cultural events.

Popular Regions:

Old Town Bari Vecchia: For a night out, the old center of Bari provides a picturesque setting. Explore the maze-like passageways to find hidden wine cellars and secret pubs in historic structures.

Lungomare: This popular promenade with restaurants, cafés, and bars is situated along the Adriatic Sea and offers breathtaking vistas in addition to a lively ambiance.

Murat District: This contemporary neighborhood is home to hip pubs, chic lounges, and exciting nightclubs. It has broad boulevards and exquisite architecture.

Bar Types:

- Customary Wine Bars: Indulge in regional delicacies and locally produced wines in little (wine bars) hidden around Bari Vecchia.
- Trendy Cocktail Bars: Take in expansive city views while sipping inventive cocktails in stylish lounges and rooftop terraces.
- Pubs and Beer Gardens: Take in the fresh air in a bustling beer garden, or unwind with a pint of craft beer in a classic pub.

Clubs:

- Demodè Club is a popular nightclub that draws a diverse population and features a variety of music genres, from house and techno to hip-hop and R&B.
- La Lampara: This legendary club, renowned for its upbeat vibe and live music events, is the perfect place to dance the night away.

Bari's nightlife offers something for everyone, whether it is a laid-back evening drinking wine in a historic setting, a vibrant night dancing to the newest sounds, or an educational experience at a theater or concert.

Lecce's Lounges and Live Music

Known as the "Florence of the South," Lecce has a sophisticated nightlife scene where excellent company, culture, and discussion are the main attractions. When the sun sets, a soft spirit emerges from the Baroque city, inviting you to discover its allure after dark.

Bars and Lounges:

Quanto Basta Bar Bar: Located amid the historic district, this trendy bar provides a well-curated wine selection, beautifully made drinks, and a fashionable environment. Unwind on luxurious couches, take in live musical acts, and socialize with the stylish set.

Bar Moro: Built-in 1909, this antique pub has a classic elegance and charm. Enjoy excellent wines, traditional drinks, and the ambiance of this iconic Lecce establishment.

Rooftop Terraces: Lecce is home to several hotels and restaurants with rooftop terraces that provide an elegant atmosphere and breathtaking views of the city's lit cityscape. Under the sky, have a nightcap or an aperitivo.

Live Music Locations:

Offside Jazz Club: Several evenings a week, local and international performers play live at this little jazz club. Sip on a bottle of wine and let the melancholic tunes carry you away.

Live music is presented on the balconies of Lecce's ancient buildings via the innovative idea of Balcony TV Lecce. Check the calendar to see what's coming up for free at a beautiful outdoor concert.

Cultural Occasions:

- Lecce Festival: This yearly summer festival features a wide variety of artistic exhibits, literary readings, theatrical productions, and concerts.
- Cinema sotto le Stelle: Throughout the summer, take advantage of free outdoor movie screenings in the city's piazzas.
- Art Openings & Exhibitions: Thanks to the city's thriving art culture, there are many opportunities to see both local and foreign artwork in Lecce. Look for exhibits and gallery openings in your area's listings.

Lecce's nightlife reflects the city's sophisticated and sophisticated attitude. You may discover a variety of alternatives to fit your taste and make an unforgettable evening, whether you're taking in live music in a historic setting, sipping a refined drink in a chic club, or participating in the city's cultural activities.

Beach Clubs and Summer Parties

Puglia's coastline turns into a playground of colorful beach clubs and throbbing summer party locations when the sun shines and the temperatures rise. Savor cool beverages, dance to the beat of the waves, and experience the carefree vibe of an Italian summer.

Salento Peninsula:

Gallipoli's Samsara Beach Located on the breathtaking Baia Verde beach, this legendary beach club is well-known for its lively ambiance, live music events, and themed parties that draw a youthful, colorful clientele.

Another well-liked destination on Baia Verde is Praja (Gallipoli). It has a sizable dance floor, many bars, and a lineup of well-known DJs playing the newest songs.

Lido Pizzo (Gallipoli): This chic beach club has a restaurant offering delectable Mediterranean food, a swimming pool, and comfy loungers for a more laid-back atmosphere.

Other Popular Beaches:

Guaia Nila (Otranto): This beach club provides a distinctive location with its private beach, lovely gardens, and a swimming pool. It is situated on the scenic Alimini Lakes. All summer long, take advantage of themed events, DJ sets, and live music.

Coco Loco (Capitolo): Located on Capitolo's sandy shoreline, this vibrant beach club is well-known for its laid-back vibe, reasonable rates, and varied clientele.

White Beach Club (Ostuni): This chic beach club, conveniently located in Ostuni, has a restaurant serving fine dining, a swimming pool, and a sophisticated setting with cozy loungers.

Tips for Taking Advantage of the Beach Club Scene:

- Reserve Early: It's best to reserve loungers and tables well in advance during the busiest months (July through August), particularly at well-known beach clubs.
- Dress Code: The majority of beach clubs have a loose dress code, but it's a beneficial idea to inquire about any special restrictions on their website or social media accounts.
- Get There Early: Arrive beforehand to get a good location by the pool or on the beach, particularly on weekends and holidays.
- Accept the Ambience: Have fun, groove to the tunes, and take in the exuberance of Puglia's summer party scene.

Puglia's beach clubs and summer party locations provide an amazing experience, whether your goal is to dance the night away beneath the stars or just unwind on a sunbed with a cool beverage.

Festivals and Events

Puglia's colorful festival scene provides an insight into the area's deep-rooted customs, fervent religious beliefs, and upbeat vibe. Ten important festivals are observed year-round and are listed below:

Festa di San Nicola (May 7–9): Notable: This large-scale celebration pays homage to St. Nicholas, the patron saint of Bari, with an enthralling fusion of religious processions, period dramas, and breathtaking fireworks. Vibe: A joyful and contemplative vibe permeates the city as residents and tourists assemble to honor the saint.

Carnevale di Putignano (December 26–Shrove Tuesday): Notable for its humorous floats, vibrant masks, and exuberant parades, Carnevale di Putignano is one of the oldest and longest-running carnivals in Italy. The town becomes a tornado of celebration, with music, dancing, and laughing filling the streets.

Melpignano's August event, Notte della Taranta, is a dynamic music festival that honors Salento's traditional Pizzica dance and folk music. It draws hundreds of passionate dancers and internationally recognized artists. The atmosphere is electrifying, with the dancers' enthusiasm and the tambourines' beat creating a memorable experience under the starry sky.

Fiera del Levante (September, Bari): Importance: The biggest trade expo in the Mediterranean, exhibiting a broad range of goods and services from different industries. The fair's atmosphere is one of innovation and business, with conferences, exhibits, and cultural activities happening throughout.

Locus Festival (Locorotondo, July–August): Importance: This well-known jazz festival draws music enthusiasts and artists from across the world to the charming village of Locorotondo, resulting in a special fusion of beautiful surroundings and captivating music. A refined and carefree vibe is produced by intimate performances in quaint settings and outdoor stages.

Festival della Valle d'Itria (Martina Franca, July–August): Noteworthy: This esteemed opera festival, housed in the venerable Palazzo Ducale, features top-notch renditions of bel canto and Baroque operas. This event draws opera lovers from all around the world with its elegant and polished style.

Cavalcade di Sant'Oronzo (Ostuni, August 25–27): Significance: Ostuni honors St. Oronzo, its patron saint, with a historic procession and an exciting horse race. There is a strong feeling of communal pride, pageantry, and traditional costumes throughout the town.

Sagra della Polpetta (Cisternino, August): Significance: This culinary celebration honors the common meatball, or "polpetta," demonstrating its delectable adaptability in a variety of dishes. As residents and guests assemble to enjoy this well-loved cuisine, a jovial and festive mood permeates the town.

Presepe Vivente (various locales, December): Significance: In Puglia, whole villages are transformed into biblical settings for an annual Christmas ritual known as "presepi," or living nativity scenes. With performers playing biblical figures and bringing the Christmas narrative to life, the atmosphere is enchanted and moving.

Celebration of Sant'Antonio Abate (January 16–17, Novoli): A huge bonfire, or "fàcara," is lit as part of this unusual celebration in honor of Saint Anthony the Abbot, the animal protector. The atmosphere is one of enthralling light and fire displays, traditional music, cuisine, and festivities.

The experience of visiting Puglia is enhanced by the lively and dynamic cultural tapestry created by these festivals and many other local events. Take part in local celebrations, get fully immersed in the area's customs, and make lifelong memories.

Theatres and performances

Beyond its festivals, Puglia has a thriving cultural sector that offers a variety of theaters and other cultural spaces where you may take in year-round engaging performances and activities.

Famous theaters and locations:

Teatro Petruzzelli (Bari): Among the biggest opera houses in Italy, this opulent venue has a varied schedule of opera, ballet, concerts, and theatrical shows.

Built in the 19th century, the Teatro Politeama Greco (Lecce) is a historic theater that hosts concerts, opera, ballet, and theatrical productions.

Opera, ballet, theater, and concerts are all included in the schedule of the classy Teatro Curci, which is situated right in the center of Barletta.

Teatro Verdi (San Severo): A variety of opera, drama, and music acts are offered in this quaint San Severo theater.

Teatro Kismet (Bari): This cutting-edge theatrical venue presents a range of modern shows, such as dance, drama, and experimental art.

The contemporary musical venue Auditorium Parco della Musica (Taranto) has a varied schedule of jazz, world music, and classical music performances.

During the summer months, Castello Svevo (Bari) organizes outdoor theater productions and concerts, offering a distinctive and evocative backdrop.

Roman Amphitheater (Lecce): A window into the city's Roman history, this historic amphitheater sits in the center of Lecce and periodically holds theatrical productions and concerts.

Types of events and performances:

- Opera: Puglia has a long history of opera, and there are annual performances at several venues.
- Ballet: Take in performances of both traditional and modern ballet at different locations.
- Theatre: Puglia's theaters provide a wide variety of theatrical experiences, ranging from contemporary shows to classic plays.
- Concerts: Attend pop, jazz, world, and classical music events in a variety of locations, such as theaters and outdoor plazas.

- Puglia has several festivals that showcase cultural activities such as dance shows, concerts, and theatrical productions.

Tips for Attending Performances:

- Ahead of time particularly for major events and peak season, check schedules and reserve tickets.
- It is particularly important to dress correctly for opera and ballet performances.
- Arrive early to secure a spot and enjoy the pre-show ambiance.
- Show consideration for both the artists and your fellow spectators.

Attending a play there is one of the best ways to soak up Puglia's rich cultural scene and make travel memories that will last a lifetime.

Chapter 6. Water Sports and Activities

Sailing and Boating

The vast coastline of Puglia, with its charming bays, quiet coves, and breathtaking islands, entices those looking for open-water experiences. Puglia offers a variety of sailing and boating activities to suit your tastes, regardless of your level of expertise or your desire for a relaxing boat ride.

Locations for Boating and Sailing:

Discover the untamed splendor of the Gargano Peninsula's shoreline, with striking cliffs, undiscovered sea caves, and glistening waves. Pass the scenic Tremiti Islands and find remote beaches that are only accessible by boat.

Salento Peninsula: Take a leisurely cruise along the breathtaking Adriatic and Ionian shores, taking in the picturesque coastal villages, white cliffs, and sandy beaches. Find secluded coves and scenic bays that are ideal for snorkeling and swimming.

Ionian Coast: Take a cruise around the serene Ionian Sea, which is renowned for its glassy waves and gorgeous sunsets. Visit the pristine beaches of the Porto Selvaggio Nature Reserve and stroll through the quaint villages of Gallipoli and Porto Cesareo.

Businesses Providing Boating and Sailing Experiences:

The Bari and Brindisi-based firm Sailing Puglia provides a variety of sailing experiences, such as day tours, sunset cruises, and multi-day sailing expeditions. They offer skippered charters and bareboat rentals, so they can accommodate both novices and seasoned sailors.

Vela Dream (Otranto, Italy): With a focus on sailing trips and courses, Vela Dream provides a range of choices to accommodate varying interests and ability levels. Take a day excursion to see Otranto's breath-taking coastline and the surrounding region, or set off on a multi-day sailing adventure to the Tremiti Islands or the Ionian Sea.

Puglia Boat Sharing (Multiple Locations): This website connects vacationers looking for shared boating experiences with boat owners. Take your pick from a range of vessels and schedules, and spend the day on the water with like-minded individuals.

Local Boat Rental Companies: You may hire a boat from a lot of the ports and marinas in Puglia and explore the coastline at your speed. Depending on your tastes and level of expertise, you may choose between motorboats, sailboats, or even classic wooden fishing vessels.

Puglia offers sailing and boating alternatives that are guaranteed to leave you with new perspectives of this stunning area and wonderful experiences, regardless of your skill level or intended experience.

Diving and Snorkeling

Underwater exploration is captivated by Puglia's rich marine habitats and crystal-clear seas. These are some of the best places to find the area's underwater wonders of the area, whether you want to scuba dive or snorkel.

Top Locations for Underwater Research:

Islands of Tremiti: Situated off the coast of the Gargano Peninsula, this archipelago is home to colorful coral reefs, underwater caverns, and shipwrecks brimming with marine life. Explore this underwater haven and come across colorful fish, octopuses, and even dolphins.

Diving Centers: On the islands, several diving centers offer a variety of levels of instruction, equipment rental, and guided dives. Prices start at around €50 per dive and vary based on the diving destination and length.

The Ionian coast's Porto Cesareo Marine Protected Area is home to a wide range of marine life, including colorful fish, dolphins, and sea turtles. Explore underwater caverns, dive or snorkel in Posidonia meadows, and take in the vibrant coral reefs.

Several Porto Cesareo diving facilities offer guided dives and snorkeling trips for both novice and expert divers. The cost varies according to the time and type of exercise.

Otranto and the shoreline around it: Divers and snorkelers may see a great deal of visibility in the crystal-clear seas around Otranto. Discover secret coves and sea caves; explore the underwater Roman remains close to the port; and see a variety of aquatic species, such as groupers, moray eels, and octopuses.

Diving Centers: In Otranto, several diving centers offer all-level training, equipment rental, and guided dives. The length and diving location affect the price.

Encounters with Marine Life:

- Vibrant fish: A rainbow of fish, such as damselfish, sea bream, parrotfish, and wrasses, should be seen.
- Cephalopods: Look for squid, cuttlefish, and octopuses that blend along with the corals and rocks.
- Crustaceans: Look for shrimp, crabs, and lobsters lurking beneath ledges and in cracks.
- Dolphins and sea turtles: In the deeper seas, intrepid snorkelers and divers could come across these magnificent animals.

Suggestions for Submerged Research:

- Select a trustworthy dive shop that offers well-kept gear and knowledgeable guides.
- Before leaving, check the sea conditions and weather.
- Please be mindful of the aquatic environment and refrain from damaging or touching any coral or marine life.
- For safety, always dive or snorkel with a companion.

The underwater environment of Puglia is a treasure trove just waiting to be explored. The area's rich marine life and breath-taking underwater scenery will wow you whether you're an experienced diver or a novice snorkeler.

Kayaking and Paddle boarding

Puglia's beautiful scenery and serene shore make it the perfect place to go kayaking and paddle boarding. Here are a few locations that are suggested:

The Porto Selvaggio Nature Reserve is situated on the Ionian shore, close to Nardò. The picturesque scenery for kayaking is created by rocky cliffs, immaculate beaches, and sheltered coves. While taking in the peace of this protected region, discover secret coves and sea caves.

The Tremiti Islands are located in the Adriatic Sea, off the Gargano Peninsula. Kayaking and paddle boarding are excellent in the tranquil seas around the islands. Discover hidden beaches, paddle among the islands, and take in the breath-taking coastline landscape.

The Porto Cesareo Marine Protected Area is situated close to Taranto on the Ionian coast. The protected area is a great place to go kayaking or paddle boarding for underwater exploration because of its tranquil waters and varied marine life. Sail across fields of sea grass, taking in the sights of vibrant fish and other aquatic life.

Varano Lake is situated close to Cagnano Varano on the Gargano Peninsula. This vast lagoon is perfect for leisurely paddling because of its quiet waters and picturesque surroundings. Explore the avian population and enjoy the tranquil ambiance.

Alimini Lakes are located on the Adriatic shore, close to Otranto. Kayaking and paddle boarding are peaceful activities on these two linked lakes. Savor the beauty of the surrounding environment and take in the variety of birds.

Advice:

Leases: Kayaks and paddleboards are easily rented at nearby beach clubs, water sports facilities, and some campgrounds.

Guided Tours: If you're new to these activities, specifically, you may want to consider taking a guided tour for a more organized and educational experience.

Safety first: wear a life jacket at all times, check the weather before you depart, and notify someone of your whereabouts and anticipated return time.

While kayaking or paddle boarding, take in the peace and beauty of Puglia's coastline and make lifelong memories at sea.

Windsurfing and Kitesurfing

Regrettably, I have no current wind and wave information for Puglia's coastline. However, I can provide you with some broad locations that are known to have favorable windsurfing and kitesurfing conditions, as well as tools to verify the conditions before you go:

General Areas:

Gargano Peninsula: notably during the summer, the northern shore of the Gargano Peninsula, especially the areas around Vieste and Peschici, is renowned for its steady winds. Kitesurfing and windsurfing are best enjoyed in circumstances created by the Tramontana (a northerly wind) and Mistral (a northwesterly wind).

Salento Peninsula: When the Scirocco, or southwest wind, blows, the southernmost point of Puglia, notably the area near Porto Cesareo and Torre San Giovanni, provides excellent windsurfing and kitesurfing conditions.

Alimini Lakes: The flat water and steady breezes of the Alimini Lakes, which are close to Otranto, make them a favorite place for windsurfing and kitesurfing.

Resources to Verify the Situation Right Now:

Windfinder: For certain places, this website and app provide comprehensive wind and weather predictions, as well as wind direction, speed, and gusts.

Windguru is another well-known resource for wind and weather predictions; it provides comparable data to Windfinder, often along with further information on wave characteristics.

Local Windsurfing and Kitesurfing Schools: The most current information on local wind and wave conditions may be found at these schools. They may also lend out equipment and provide instruction.

Important Reminder:

- Since the wind and weather may change suddenly, always check the most recent information before leaving.
- Determine your ability level and pick a place that is appropriate for you.
- Put on the proper protective clothing, such as a helmet and life jacket.
- If you've never played these sports before, think about enrolling in classes with a trained teacher.

You may have a thrilling and risk-free windsurfing or kitesurfing experience in Puglia if you pay attention to these pointers and select the ideal spot depending on the weather at the time.

Fishing Trips

For anglers of all skill levels, Puglia's vast coastline and varied marine environments provide excellent chances. Here are some suggested sites and fishing experiences, ranging from relaxing seaside outings to exhilarating deep-sea adventures:

Coastal Fishing:

Gargano Peninsula: Rock fishing and beach casting is excellent on the untamed Gargano Peninsula's craggy coastlines and secluded bays. Target species include mullet, sea bass, and sea bream.

Salento Peninsula: With its sandy beaches and rocky outcrops, Puglia's southernmost point provides a variety of fishing options. For mackerel, sea bass, and sea bream, cast your line.

Otranto and the Adriatic Coast: Bottom and light tackle fishing are excellent in the crystal-clear waters around these locations. Seek for fish species such as sea bream, scorpion fish, and red mullet.

Deep Sea Fishing:

Exciting deep-sea fishing trips may be had by traveling to the Tremiti Islands for deep-sea fishing. Aim for bigger species such as mahi-mahi, swordfish, and tuna.

Gallipoli and the Ionian Coast: The Ionian Sea provides prospects for deep-sea fishing excursions, with the possibility of catching amberjack, swordfish, and tuna.

Different Experiences with Fishing:

- Traditional Fishing with Locals: Take a unique trip with local fishermen to discover their fishing methods and learn about the area's fishing culture.
- Guided Fishing Tours: Go fishing with knowledgeable captains who will show you the best places to fish and provide all the gear you need.
- Charters for Private Boats: Hire a private boat and personalize your fishing trip by selecting the spots and fishing techniques that you like.
- Shore Fishing: Cast your line from rocky outcrops or lovely beaches, and enjoy a leisurely day of fishing from the shore.

Particular Suggestions:

Sea bream, sea bass, and tuna may be caught in the coastal and deep-water fishing grounds of Trani and Bisceglie, two quaint fishing villages along the Adriatic coast.

Torre Canne: This seaside town is well-known for its fantastic fishing spots, which provide both on-shore and offshore fishing options. Red mullet, sea bass, and sea bream are among the target species.

Otranto: Take a guided fishing excursion to discover the Adriatic Sea's abundant marine life and try your hand at catching a variety of species from Otranto.

Before you cast your line, don't forget to verify the local fishing rules and get any required permissions. For those looking for peace and adventure while fishing, Puglia is a fishing haven with its many waterways and varied fishing opportunities.

Chapter 7: Museums and Galleries

Archaeological Museums

With its diverse historical and cultural heritage, Puglia is home to many well-known museums that provide insightful looks into the region's history and present. The famous bronze figure known as the "Athlete of Taranto" is one of the many amazing objects on display at the Archaeological Museum in Bari, which spans the prehistoric to Roman eras. The museum costs €6 to enter and is open Tuesday through Sunday from 8:30 AM to 7:30 PM.

The Museo Storico della Città di Lecce (MUST) in Lecce uses artifacts from the Middle Ages, Baroque masterpieces, and archeological discoveries to tell the story of the city's past. The museum costs €5 to enter and is located in the 16th-century Palazzo Turrisi. It is open Tuesday through Sunday from 9:00 AM to 7:00 PM.

Magna Graecia antiquities abound in Taranto's National Archaeological Museum (MArTA), which is home to the magnificent "Ori di Taranto" (Gold of Taranto) collection. The museum has an entry fee of €8 and is open Tuesday through Sunday from 8:30 a.m. to 7:30 p.m.

The Pinacoteca Provinciale di Bari, housed in the 17th-century Palazzo della Provincia, has a collection of paintings spanning the 14th and 20th centuries, including pieces by well-known Puglian painters. The museum is free to enter and is open Tuesday through Sunday from 9:00 AM to 7:00 PM.

The Museo della Civiltà Contadina (Museum of Peasant Civilization) in Alberobello, situated in a trullo, offers a unique experience. With displays of home goods, agricultural implements, and traditional clothing, it provides a window into Puglia's traditional rural way of life. The museum charges a €3 entry fee and is open every day from 9:00 AM to 6:00 PM.

Art Galleries

With a variety of galleries exhibiting both traditional and modern work, Puglia's art scene is thriving and gives both established and up-and-coming artists a platform. Here are some galleries you should check out:

Polignano a Mare, Fondazione Museo Pino Pascali: This museum, which is devoted to the well-known Puglian artist Pino Pascali, features both temporary exhibits of modern art and his inventive works. Its distinctive location—a slaughterhouse from the 17th century—adds to the experience. Open from 10:00 AM to 1:00 PM and 5:00 PM to 8:00 PM, Tuesday through Sunday. €5 admission.

Galleria Nazionale della Puglia (Bitonto): This national gallery has a sizable collection of Medieval and 20th-century Puglian art, housed in a palace from the 15th century. Explore the area's creative development and admire regional masters' creations. Monday through Sunday, 8:30 a.m. to 7:30 p.m. €4 admission.

Museo Sigismondo Castromediano (Lecce): Set in a former monastery, this museum features a wide range of artistic and archeological artifacts, from Baroque paintings and sculptures from the Middle Ages to modern pieces. Discover Puglia's creative legacy by browsing through its numerous parts. Open 9:00 AM to 8:00 PM, Tuesday through Sunday.

Spezio Murat (Bari): This modern art venue has a varied schedule of exhibits, installations, and performances that highlight the work of both renowned and up-and-coming artists. Admission is €5. It's a thriving center for cross-cultural dialogue and innovation. Depending on the show, different opening times and entry costs apply.

Galleria Contemporanea di Arte (Lecce): This gallery features pieces by both domestic and foreign artists to support current art. Explore innovative paintings, sculptures, installations, and multimedia works. Depending on the show, opening times and entry costs may change.

These galleries provide an intriguing look into Puglia's creative scene, as do the many smaller independent locations dotted across the area. Every art enthusiast will find something to inspire and enthrall them, whether they are traditional crafts or modern interpretations.

Historical Palaces and Castles

The region's rich and complex history is reflected in the abundance of castles and palaces dotting the region's landscape. These magnificent buildings provide tourists with an insight into the lifestyles of former monarchs, the architectural styles of different times, and the strategic significance of Puglia throughout the centuries.

Alexandria's Castel del Monte: Constructed by Emperor Frederick II in the 13th century, this famous fortress is well-known for its unusual octagonal architecture and enigmatic function. It is a symbol of the emperor's imaginative spirit and the medieval magnificence of Puglia, and it is recognized as a UNESCO World Heritage Site.

Formerly a Norman stronghold, Castello Svevo (Bari) is an impressive 12th-century fortress that was essential to the city's security. Today, guests are free to tour the ramparts, courtyards, and vast halls while taking in the striking combination of Angevin, Swabian, and Norman architectural designs.

Castello Aragonese (Otranto): Located on the Adriatic coast, is a magnificent fortification from the 15th century that was a vital barrier against Ottoman invasions. Its commanding position and massive construction provide insight into Otranto's stormy history and its function in the area's defence,

Palazzo Ducale (Martina Franca): This graceful 17th-century palace, which was once the Dukes of Martina Franca's home, is a magnificent example of the area's Baroque architectural beauty. Its opulent halls, elaborate murals, and lovely courtyard whisk guests back in time to a time of immense wealth and grandeur.

Castello di Trani: Built on a peninsula overlooking the Adriatic Sea, is a marvel of medieval architecture dating back to the 13th century. Its significance in protecting Trani City is seen in its advantageous position and strong defences.

Puglia is home to a vast array of palaces and castles, to name a few. Every one of them provides a different perspective on the intriguing history of the area, enticing tourists to go back in time and get engrossed in the myths and tales that have molded its character. These historical sites are guaranteed to make an impact, whether you're exploring their towering walls, appreciating their architectural intricacies, or just taking in the expansive vistas they have to offer.

Specialized Museums

Puglia has a variety of specialist museums that appeal to a wide range of interests, in addition to the conventional art and history museums. These distinctive establishments provide a more thorough exploration of certain subjects, offering enlightening perspectives and rewarding experiences.

The Museo della Civiltà Contadina (Museum of Peasant Civilization) in Alberobello is located in a quaint Trullo and offers visitors a look into Puglian rural life in the past. View displays of domestic goods, agricultural implements, traditional attire, and relics from handicrafts and agriculture. Opening times usually open Monday through Friday from 9:00 AM to 6:00 PM, however for the most up-to-date information, see their website. To gain access, a small fee, often approximately €3, is required.

The Confetti Museum, or Museo del Confetto, is located in the center of Andria and honors the craft of producing confetti, which is a highly valued Puglian heritage. Discover the background of confetti, see the elaborate production process, and be amazed by the vibrant arrangements of beautiful sugar-coated almonds. Hours of Operation is usually Monday through Friday, 9:00 AM to 1:00 PM and 3:00 PM to 7:00 PM. Entry is subject to a nominal fee, typically about €5.

The Olive Oil Museum, or Museo dell'Olio, is situated in the Masseria S. Angelo de' Graecis in Fasano. It delves into the history and production of olive oil, which is essential to Puglian food and culture. View displays that highlight antique olive presses, customary implements, and the development of methods for producing olive oil. Operating hours start from 9:00 AM - 1:00 PM and 3:00 PM - 6:00 PM, Monday through Friday.

Saturdays and Sundays exclusively with prior reservations and there is no entry fee.

The Museum of the Water, or Museo del Mare, is located in Taranto and investigates the area's nautical history and its connection to the water. It is housed in the Aragonese Castle. See displays on maritime life, shipbuilding, fishing customs, and underwater archeology. Opening hours start from 8:30 AM to 7:30 PM, Tuesday through Sunday. Part of the €8 adult ticket (€2 for students), which includes admission to the Aragonese Castle.

Museo della Cartapesta (Papier-Mâché Museum) - Lecce: This museum honors the craft of papier-mâché, a treasured custom in the city, and is situated in Lecce. Take in the elaborate and vibrant papier-mâché works, which include anything from amusing creatures to religious figures and ornamental items. Hours of Operation start from 9:00 AM to 7:00 PM every day. Entry is subject to a nominal cost, often around €3.

These specialist museums provide one-of-a-kind and captivating experiences that let guests learn more about certain facets of Puglia's customs, history, and culture. Any interest in olive oil, confetti, maritime history, or traditional crafts may be satiated by visiting one of Puglia's museums, which can enhance your knowledge of this intriguing area.

Chapter 8: Day Trips and Excursions

Matera

Travelers are drawn to Matera, a UNESCO World Heritage Site, by its fascinating prehistoric cave homes known as the "Sassi." This unusual settlement offers a glimpse into a world where time seems to have stopped still, created from the untamed environment of Basilicata. Matera's alluring appeal may be fully experienced with a day excursion from Puglia.

Why Matera?

The Sassi: These prehistoric cave homes, occupied since the Paleolithic period, are evidence of the inventiveness and tenacity of the human race. Explore the winding alleyways, be in awe of the cave churches, and take in this amazing place's distinct ambiance.

Magnificent Views: Take in expansive views of the Sassi and surrounding areas from the Piazza Duomo panoramic terrace or the Belvedere overlook.

Immersion in Culture: Matera's history, customs, and culture are rich. Take some time to visit its artisan studios, museums, and cathedrals to learn more about this intriguing city.

Practical Advice for a One-Day Trip:

- Transportation: A bus or rail from Puglia to Matera is an effortless journey. From Bari, the trip takes one and a half to two hours. It's a beneficial idea to get tickets in advance, particularly during busy times.
- Tours with Guides: To understand the historical and cultural importance of the Sassi and its cave churches, it is strongly advised that you take a guided tour. Select a tour based on your time limits and areas of interest.
- Wear Comfortable Shoes: As you visit the Sassi, be ready to walk on rough ground and climb stairs.
- Water and Snacks: Keep yourself hydrated and well-fed while exploring by packing a drink and snacks.
- Timing: To avoid crowds and make the most of your day, schedule your arrival for early in the morning.

A day excursion to Matera provides a one-of-a-kind and spectacular experience that transports one back in time. With a little forethought and preparation, you can easily visit this fascinating city and create treasured memories of your Puglian vacation.

Islands of Tremiti

A sanctuary of peace and natural beauty, the Tremiti Islands are an archipelago off the coast of Puglia, tucked in the Adriatic Sea. The stunning combination of immaculate beaches, glistening oceans, verdant greenery, and striking cliffs can be found on these five islands: San Domino, San Nicola, Capraia, Cretaccio, and Pianosa.

Natural Beauty:

San Domino: The biggest and most populous island in the archipelago, San Domino is home to Cala Arena, the only sandy beach in the archipelago, as well as verdant pine trees and quiet coves. Its scenic terrain begs for exploration by bicycle or foot.

San Nicola: Situated on a cliff, this picturesque community is surrounded by a medieval abbey. Take in the expansive vistas, stroll around the island's winding lanes, and take in the peace.

The deserted islands of Capraia, Cretaccio, and Pianosa provide a window into Puglia's wild interior. Discover their rocky shores, take in the variety of birds, and unearth secret grottoes and caverns.

Activities:

- Boat Tours: Take a boat excursion across the archipelago to see the beautiful rock formations, sea caves, and undiscovered bays. Take in the vivid marine life by diving or snorkeling in the pristine seas.
- Swimming and Sunbathing: Take a leisurely swim and sunbathe on the sandy beaches of San Domino, or find a quiet cove on one of the other islands.

- Hiking & Nature Walks: Take beautiful routes that meander through woods, along cliffs, and to secret views to discover the islands' varied flora and wildlife.
- Discover the beautiful coral reefs, underwater caverns, and shipwrecks brimming with marine life in the Tremiti Islands by scuba diving and snorkeling.
- Kayaking and paddleboarding: Take in the peace and beauty as you glide across the serene seas that round the islands.
- Birdwatching: note the many avian species, such as cormorants, seagulls, and uncommon migrating birds.

The Tremiti Islands provide a tranquil haven away from the mainland where you may take in the splendor of nature, engage in a range of outdoor activities, and make lifelong memories. Every tourist may find something to enjoy in this oasis on the Adriatic, whether they are looking for adventure, leisure, or a mix of the two.

National Park of Gargano

Hikers are welcome to explore the varied landscapes of Puglia's northern tip, Gargano National Park, which spans vast wilderness areas with stunning cliffs, rough coasts, and deep woods.

Trails:

Foresta Umbra: A network of pathways meanders among towering trees and rich foliage in this old beech forest, which is recognized as a UNESCO World Heritage Site. As you stroll through this lush reserve, you may come across rare orchids, deer, and wild boar.

Sentiero dei Due Golfi: This expansive path that links Peschici and Vieste provides breathtaking views of the two gulfs that round the Gargano Peninsula, as well as the Adriatic Sea.

Hiking from Monte Sant'Angelo to Mattinata is strenuous, but the rewards include breathtaking views of the coastline and the Tremiti Islands. As you stroll through olive trees, historic towns, and striking cliffs, you can fully appreciate the park's breathtaking scenery.

Scenic Viewpoints:

- Punta Lunga: This viewpoint, which is close to Vieste, provides panoramic views of the Adriatic Sea, the Tremiti Islands, and the untamed Gargano coastline.
- Torre dell'Orso: From this point of view near Melendugno, take in the striking cliffs, the white sand beach, and the famous sea stacks known as "Le Due Sorelle" (the Two Sisters).
- Monte Calvo: Achieve sweeping views of the Adriatic Sea and the whole peninsula by climbing Monte Calvo, the highest peak in the Gargano.

Flora and Fauna:

Various Ecosystems the park's diverse topography is home to a wide variety of plants and animals. Discover rare orchids, aromatic Mediterranean scrub, and old-growth beech woods.

Animals: See foxes, deer, wild boar, and an array of avian species, such as owls, hawks, and eagles. Marine life and seabirds enjoy a sanctuary at the Tremiti Islands.

Hikers may interact with the untamed beauty of the area and unearth its hidden gems in Gargano National Park, which provides an immersive natural experience.

Valle d'Itria Cycling

In the charming Itria Valley of Puglia, where undulating hills, vineyards, and recognizable trulli provide a gorgeous background for amazing cycling journeys, embrace the slow pace of life. As you cycle through this picturesque terrain, you'll come across hidden treasures, quaint towns, and beautiful views.

Beautiful Routes:

The Trail of Trulli: This well-traveled path connects the villages of Alberobello, Locorotondo, and Martina Franca by circling in the center of the Itria Valley. Enjoy the distinct charm of the area as you pedal by many trulli, vineyards, and olive trees.

Cisternino to Ostuni: From the quaint village of Cisternino, take this picturesque road to reach the brilliant white city of Ostuni, which is well-known for its "Fornelli Pronti" (butcher shops with on-site grilling). Bike through vineyards and olive orchards, taking in expansive views of the Adriatic Sea and the surrounding area.

The Adriatic Coast: For a thrilling seaside journey, cycle from Monopoli south to Polignano a Mare along the Adriatic Sea. Along the route, take in the breathtaking views of the sea, scenic cliffs, and quaint fishing towns.

Options for Renting:

Local Bike stores: You may hire a range of bikes in the Itria Valley, including city bikes, mountain bikes, and e-bikes, from several bike stores located in various towns. Usually, prices go from €15 to €25 per day.

Guided Bike Tours: To discover the valley, take a guided bike trip with an experienced local guide. These trips often include stops at vineyards, mills that make olive oil, and other intriguing locations.

Scenic Highlights:

- Trulli: Stroll by many trulli and take in their distinct design and elegance as they are painted white.
- Olive Groves and Vineyards: As you bike past seemingly endless fields of olive trees and vineyards, take in the tranquil countryside atmosphere.

- Hilltop Towns: Get to know little communities with unique personalities and attractions, such as Locorotondo, Martina Franca, and Cisternino.
- Panoramic Views: Scale the slopes to get amazing views of the surrounding landscape, the Adriatic Sea, and the valley.
- Local food: Along the route, make sure to stop at family-run trattorias and rural farmhouses to enjoy delectable Puglian food.

Riding a bicycle in the Itria Valley is an exquisite experience that presents a distinct viewpoint of the area's gastronomic pleasures, cultural legacy, and scenic splendor. The valley's mild inclines and well-kept roads make it a wonderful place for a two-wheeled adventure, regardless of your level of experience.

Wine Tours and Tastings

The wine industry in Puglia is booming, and more and more vineyards are providing tourists with distinctive experiences. Here are some suggestions for enjoying the region's many vintages:

The famous Tormaresca Winery (Minervino Murge & San Pietro Vernotico), which has properties in both northern and southern Puglia, offers guided tours and wine tastings of its award-winning wines, including the famed Bocca di Lupo Castel del Monte DOCG and the sophisticated Chardonnay Salento IGT. While taking in the breathtaking views of the vineyard, discover their sustainable winemaking methods.

Cantine Due Palme (Cellino San Marco): Visit this family-run vineyard to get a true sense of the Primitivo region. Enjoy a sampling of their superb Primitivo di Manduria DOC wines, which include the flagship Selvarossa, and take a tour of the vineyards and cellars.

Tenute Rubino (Brindisi): This cutting-edge winery provides a unique "wine experience" that mixes wine tastings with regional cuisine and cultural events. It is situated close to the Adriatic coast. Take a taste of Puglian delicacies, learn about their biodynamic agricultural methods, and visit their vineyards.

Situated in the scenic Itria Valley, Cantina Cardone (Locorotondo) is a winery that specializes in white wines, namely the Verdeca and Locorotondo DOC grape types. Enjoy a tasting of their crisp, light wines, as well as a guided tour of the vineyards and cellars.

Nestled between olive orchards and vineyards, Masseria Li Veli (Cellino San Marco) provides a distinctive wine-tasting experience in a picturesque rural environment. Savor their award-winning organic wines, such as Susumaniello, and take in a leisurely lunch in their classic restaurant.

Wine Tours by Bike or Vespa: Several tour companies provide guided wine tours by bike or Vespa, which let you see many vineyards in a single day while exploring the gorgeous countryside. Ride or pedal through quaint towns, vineyards, and olive groves, stopping along the way to taste regional wines and take in the beauty.

Tips for Choosing a Wine Tour or Tasting:

- Think about your hobbies: Which kind of winery—a bigger, more established one or a smaller, family-run one—do you prefer? Do you want to know more about creating wine using organic or biodynamic methods?
- Examine the available options: Do they offer guided cellar and vineyard tours? Which kinds of tastings are offered? Do meal pairings get included?
- Make reservations in advance: It's advisable to reserve your wine tour or tasting in advance to assure availability, especially during busy times of the year.
- Travel: Take into account your options for getting to and from the vineyard. Certain wineries' tour packages include transportation as a perk.

Discovering Puglia's diversified wine industry will help you understand the region's rich viticultural legacy and the passion of its winemakers, in addition to helping you find outstanding wines.

Chapter 9: Beyond the Guidebook

Hidden Gems and Off-the-Beaten-Path

Puglia offers a multitude of lesser-known locations and experiences that are sure to pique your curiosity and leave you with lifelong memories, perfect for the adventurous traveler looking to explore beyond the beaten roads.

Grotta della Poesia (Roca Vecchia): Tucked away on the Adriatic coast, this natural swimming hole is sculpted into limestone cliffs. Take a dip in the azure waters, investigate the nearby caverns, and take in the spectacular view.

Torre Sant'Andrea: Sea stacks magnificent rock formations, and naturally occurring arches sculpted by the unrelenting waves may all be seen in Torre Sant'Andrea, a breath-taking coastal location close to Otranto. Discover secluded coves and immaculate beaches as you stroll or cruise the craggy shoreline.

Cisternino: Often overlooked by its more well-known neighbors, this quaint hilltop village provides a window into real Puglian life. Explore its maze-like passageways, indulge in mouthwatering grilled meats at a "fornello pronto," and take in the cozy ambiance of its medieval setting.

Puglian Gravina is a historic village situated atop a ravine. It is home to an intriguing network of churches, bridges, and cave homes that cross the stunning chasm. Walk along the ravine's edge, see its historic core, and take in the breathtaking vistas.

Grotte di Castellana: Explore the magical subterranean world of the Castellana Caves, a sophisticated system of stalactites, stalagmites, and subterranean lakes. Take a guided tour to learn about this natural wonder and its geological structures.

Salina dei Monaci Nature Reserve: This protected wetland region near Manduria provides a rare chance to study salt marsh ecology and witness a variety of birds. Take a walk along the paths, see flamingos and other migrating birds, and see how salt is traditionally made.

Pizzomunno Beach in Vieste is a secret haven on the Gargano Peninsula that can only be reached by boat or a steep stairway. Unwind on its silky beaches, take a dip in its glistening waters, and take in the famous Pizzomunno sea stack—a legendary natural landmark.

These are only a few of the many off-the-beaten-path experiences Puglia has to offer. Accept the spirit of adventure, go beyond your comfort zone, and unearth the hidden gems of the area.

Responsible Travel and Sustainability

Puglia's natural beauty and cultural legacy are crucial to the region's long-term viability. During your stay, you can reduce your environmental affect and show support for the local community by doing the following:

Reduce the Impact on the Environment:

- Trim, Reuse, and Recycle Adopt the 3 R's: reduce trash, reuse containers, and recycle as much as you can.
- Preserve Water: Use water carefully, particularly in the sweltering summer months. When not in use, turn off the faucets, take shorter showers, and report any leaks.
- Respect the Environment: When hiking or visiting natural areas, stay on approved pathways. Don't disturb animals, and leave no evidence of your visit.
- Select Sustainable transit: Whenever feasible, use walking, cycling, or public transit. Think about renting an electric or hybrid automobile.
- Encourage Eco-Friendly Accommodations: Pick lodgings that emphasize sustainable practices, such as those that have recycling initiatives, water conservation measures, and renewable energy sources.

Encourage your local communities:

- Shop local: Support your community's economy and help preserve traditional crafts by purchasing gifts and souvenirs from nearby stores and artists.
- Eat at Local Restaurants: Support small businesses and the local culinary culture by indulging in real Puglian cuisine at family-run trattorias and restaurants.

- Engage Locals: Learn about the locals' customs and lifestyle and respect their culture.
- Learn a Few words: Expressing interest in the local language and fostering relationships may be accomplished with only a few simple Italian words.
- Donate or Volunteer: If you want to help local groups that promote community development or environmental protection, think about making a donation or offering your time.

You can help ensure that Puglia's dynamic towns, natural beauty, and cultural history are preserved for future generations to enjoy by practicing responsible travel.

Tips for Travelers

Cultural Standards:

Dress Code: Although most venues allow casual wear, when visiting churches or other places of worship, wear modest clothing. Keep beachwear off in town centres.

Salutations: Saying "Buongiorno" (good morning/day) or "Buonasera" (good evening) with friendliness makes a big difference. When you first meet someone, you usually shake hands, and friends and acquaintances typically plant cheek kisses.

Tipping: Although not required, gratuities are appreciated for excellent service. In restaurants, leave a tiny bit of cash or round up the bill.

Meal Times: Usually consumed between 1:00 PM and 3:00 PM, lunch is the primary meal of the day. Usually eaten later in the evening, about 8:00 or 9:00 PM, dinner is milder in flavor.

Packing Advice:

- Comfy Shoes: Since you'll probably be wandering about a lot, bring comfy walking shoes.
- Beach Essentials & Swimwear: Bring sunscreen, a beach towel, and swimwear if you're coming during the warmer months.
- Layers: Bring clothing appropriate for changing climates, particularly if you're traveling in the winter or shoulder seasons.
- Adapters: Two-pin European plugs are used in Italy; if needed, carry an adaptor.

Security:

- Petty Theft: Take extra care with your possessions in busy places and popular tourist destinations. Refrain from carrying a lot of cash, and safeguard your valuables.
- Scams: Keep an eye out for typical travel scams, such as phony petitions or diversion. Make use of trustworthy transportation providers and tour operators.

- Driving: Use caution while driving and pay attention to the local driving customs. In some places, roads may be twisting and narrow.
- Emergency Numbers: To contact police, fire, or ambulance services in an emergency, call 112.

A comfortable and pleasurable vacation to Puglia may be guaranteed by following basic safety measures, packing sensibly, and honoring local traditions. Accept the distinctive culture of the area and make lifelong memories.

Planning Your Itinerary

Several example itineraries that accommodate varying interests and trip lengths are provided below to help you plan your vacation to Puglia:

Cultural and Historical Background Buff (7 days):

- Day 1–2: Take a tour of Bari, stopping in Bari Vecchia, Castello Svevo, and the Basilica di San Nicola.
- Day 3-4: Immerse yourself in the Baroque splendor of Lecce by visiting its piazzas, churches, and Roman Amphitheater.
- Day 5–6: Along the way, visit Locorotondo and Martina Franca as you meander about Ostuni's whitewashed alleyways, taking in the allure of the Itria Valley.
- Day 7: Spend the day in Matera and learn about the Sassi's fascinating past.

Seven-day Beach and Relaxation Seeker:

- Day 3–7: Recuperate on the immaculate Salento beaches while lodging in Otranto or Gallipoli. Admire boat rides and discover communities along the shore.
- Day 4-5: Take in the allure of Polignano a Mare and Monopoli, with their gorgeous beaches and cliffside vistas.
- Day 6-7: Unwind with spa treatments and poolside relaxation in an opulent Masseria in the countryside.

Wine and Food Connoisseur (5 days):

- Day 1–2: Learn about Bari's gastronomic scene by visiting its markets and trying local cuisine.
- Day 3: Go on an Itria Valley wine tour, stopping at nearby vineyards and indulging in sampling.
- Day 4: Learn how to make traditional Puglian food by enrolling in a Masseria cooking session.
- Day 5: Savor Lecce's gastronomic joys by visiting its thriving food markets and savoring regional delicacies.

Nature enthusiast and outdoor explorer (5 days):

- Day 1–2: Take a hike in the Gargano National Park and take in the varied scenery and beautiful routes.
- Day 3: Ride your bike across the lovely Itria Valley, stopping at quaint villages and breathtaking views.

- Day 4: Paddle a kayak or a paddleboard in the serene seas of the Tremiti Islands or Porto Selvaggio Nature Reserve.
- Day 5: Take it leisurely and enjoy the sun and water while lounging on the beaches of Otranto or Torre Guaceto Nature Reserve.

These are just a handful of illustrations to get you thinking. You are welcome to combine and contrast places and activities to design an itinerary that precisely fits your schedule and interests. Always keep in mind that the secret to a fulfilling and joyful trip is flexibility.

Essential Packing List

Puglia's various activities and sceneries need a well-thought-out packing list. Considering the season and the activities you have scheduled, here are the essential things to make sure you're ready for your Puglian adventure:

Basic Needs:

- Visa and passport (if needed): Make sure that the duration of your planned stay on your passport is at least three months. Verify the prerequisites for a visa well in advance.
- Travelers' Insurance: To pay for unforeseen medical costs, trip cancellations, or misplaced baggage, comprehensive travel insurance is essential.

- Comfortable Walking Shoes: Since you'll be walking about a lot, bring sturdy and comfy shoes.
- Adapters: If your gadgets don't fit the two-pin European plugs used in Italy, remember to include one.
- Puglia has plenty of sunlight, so wear sunscreen, a hat, and sunglasses to protect yourself.
- Reusable Water Bottle: Carrying a reusable water bottle can help you stay hydrated and reduce plastic waste.
- First-Aid Kit: Stock up on basic first-aid supplies, such as band-aids, painkillers, and antihistamines.

Seasonal Considerations:

- Summer (June-August): Bring a swimsuit, a beach towel, a sun hat, and lightweight, breathable clothes. In the evenings and air-conditioned areas, wear a lightweight shawl or scarf.
- Autumn/Spring (April-May, September-October): Pack layers, such as lightweight sweaters, long-sleeved shirts, and a jacket for chilly nights. It's also advised to have an umbrella or rain jacket.
- Winter (November–March): Bring layers of warm clothes, such as trousers, sweaters, and water-resistant jackets. It will also be helpful to have a hat, gloves, and scarf.

Items Particular to an Activity:

- Hiking: Bring a map or GPS device, a backpack, and strong hiking boots if you're planning treks in the Gargano National Park or other locations.
- Cycle: You may want to pack gloves, a helmet, and cycle shorts if you want to ride in the Itria Valley or another location.
- Beach Activities: If you want to explore rocky coasts, bring water shoes, a beach bag, a beach towel, and a swimsuit.
- If you're thinking of going diving or snorkeling, bring your equipment, or ask your dive facility about rentals.

Extra Things:

- Phrasebook or App for Translation: Even if there are tourist destinations where English is widely spoken, using a phrasebook or translation tool might help you communicate with locals.
- Camera: Use your smartphone's lens or a camera to record Puglia's breath-taking landscape and special moments.
- Travel Journal: To make a permanent memento of your journey, jot down your experiences, ideas, and impressions in a travel journal.

Always emphasize wearing adaptable, mix-and-match apparel, and travel light. You'll be ready to fully enjoy your Puglian journey if you pack sensibly and take the activities and season into account.

Chapter 10: Additional Resources

Useful Websites and Apps

Websites:

The official Italy tourism website, Italia it has extensive information about every area of the country, including Puglia. Discover information on travel-related activities, events, transportation, and attractions.

Puglia Promozione (Official Tourism Board of Puglia): This website provides comprehensive guidance on locations, activities, itineraries, and events, along with special information about Puglia.

Viaggiareinpuglia.it: This website, which offers details on lodging, dining options, events, and local experiences, is yet another useful tool for organizing your vacation to Puglia.

The Thinking Traveller: This opulent villa rental business provides carefully chosen itineraries and insider knowledge on Puglia, including off-the-beaten-path excursions and hidden treasures.

Apps:

- Trenitalia: You can look up train timetables, buy tickets, and get up-to-date travel information on this official app from the Italian National Railway.
- TheFork: This app assists you in finding and reserving restaurants in Puglia, often with exclusive deals and discounts.
- Google Maps: An essential tool for travel, Maps lets you plan routes, locate public transit, and identify local attractions.
- Duolingo: Improve your knowledge of Italian with this free language-learning program.

Extra Sources:

- Local Tourist Information Offices: For maps, brochures, and insider information, stop by the tourist information offices in the towns and cities you want to visit.
- Travel Blogs and resources: A wealth of web resources and travel blogs provide insightful analysis and suggestions about Puglia.
- Social media: For inspiration and the most recent news on events and activities, follow Puglia-related accounts on Facebook and Instagram.

With these tools, you'll be ready to organize a rewarding and unforgettable vacation to Puglia. Remember that exploring off the beaten route and finding hidden treasures often results in the finest vacation experiences. Accept the adventurer's mindset, mingle with the people, and let Puglia's enchantment reveal itself to you.

Recommended Books and Films

To further your knowledge and enjoyment of Puglia's many cultures, histories, and landscapes, you may want to watch or read the following movies or books:

Books:

Carlo Levi's nonfiction work "Christ Stopped at Eboli" describes his experiences as a political exile living in a secluded community in the Puglia region of Basilicata. It provides a moving look into the area's early 20th-century rural lifestyle and cultural customs.

Chris Harrison's book "Head over Heel: Seduced by Southern Italy": This book, which is chock-full of funny tales and perceptive insights on the people and way of life in Puglia, follows the author's journey of self-discovery and cultural immersion.

Tom Mueller's engrossing book "Extra Virginity: The Sublime and Scandalous World of Olive Oil" explores the history, cultural relevance, and current issues of the olive oil business. A must-read for all those who are curious about Puglia's "liquid gold."

Helena Attlee's exquisitely written book, "The Land Where Lemons Grow: The Story of Italy and its Citrus Fruit," delves into the cultural importance and history of Italian citrus fruits, emphasizing Puglia's role in their production and culinary applications.

Ursula Ferrigno's booklet "Puglia: Recipes from Italy's Heel" offers a variety of traditional Puglian recipes, from traditional pasta meals and seafood specialties to rustic vegetable stews and mouth-watering desserts.

Movies:

1988's "Cinema Paradiso": Giuseppe Tornatore's endearing Italian film recounts the tale of a little child in a tiny Sicilian town who has a passion for movies. It's not set in Puglia, yet it conveys the essence of the region and its ageless customs.

"Io non ho " (I'm Not Scared) (2003): Set in the remote Puglian countryside, this gripping Italian thriller has a director, Gabriele Salvatores. It deals with issues like friendship, innocence in childhood, and the darker side of human nature.

(2010) "Mine vaganti" (Loose Cannons): Under the direction of Ferzan Özpetek, this Italian comedy-drama narrates the tale of a young guy who struggles to come out as gay when he returns to his family in Salento. It provides an insight into the changing social dynamics of modern Puglian society.

"6 underground" (2019): Shot in Matera and the surrounding countryside, this action-packed Hollywood thriller directed by Michael Bay showcases the spectacular scenery of the area.

By providing a window into Puglia's rich culture, history, and landscapes, these books and movies will enhance your trip and strengthen your bond with this alluring area.

Local Contacts and Emergency Information

Even if we hope that your vacation to Puglia is full of unforgettable moments, it's a beneficial idea to be ready for any unanticipated events. The following are crucial phone numbers and resources to have on hand in case of emergency:

Emergency phone numbers:

Emergency Situation:

- 112 (You may reach the police, fire, or ambulance services by calling this number.)
- Police: 113
- Fire: 115
- 118 ambulances

Vital Contacts:

- Your Consulate or Embassy: Get in touch with your Italian embassy or consulate in the event of a passport loss or theft, severe sickness, or other emergency.
- Local tourist information offices may help with lost items, general questions, and other non-emergency circumstances.

Extra Sources:

- Nearby hospitals Find out the addresses and phone numbers of the hospitals in the places you want to visit, particularly if you have any medical history.
- Pharmacies: note the addresses of the pharmacies close to your lodging in case you need to buy prescription drugs or need help.
- Travel Insurance Provider: Have your travel insurance provider's contact details handy in case you need to file a claim.

General Safety Advice:

- Pay attention to your surroundings, particularly in busy places and popular tourist destinations.
- Steer clear of flashing expensive stuff or carrying big sums of cash.
- Make use of trustworthy travel companies and transportation providers.
- When swimming or engaging in other water sports, use caution.
- Observe local laws and traditions.

Being organized and having these crucial connections and tools at your disposal will help you travel more peacefully and guarantee a fun and safe time in Puglia. Recall that taking a few extra precautions might help to ensure a worry-free journey.

Dear Reader

Thank you for choosing Puglia Travel Guide as your companion on this journey. I hope the insights, tips, and stories within these pages have enriched your experience and sparked a deeper love for Puglian's rich culture and breath-taking landscapes.

Your feedback is invaluable to me. If you enjoyed this guide and found it helpful, I would greatly appreciate it if you could take a moment to leave a positive review. Your thoughts not only help other travelers discover this book but also inspire me to continue sharing the wonders of the world through my writing.

Thank you for being a part of this adventure. I wish you safe travels and unforgettable memories.

Warm regards,

Glen C. Flores

Made in the USA
Las Vegas, NV
19 October 2024

10091767R00075